CH

D0623731

Westminster Public Library
Damaged prior to: 03.04.18
Damage noted: Brown Stains Am.

DISCARD
WESTMINSTER PUBLIC LIBRARY
3031 WEST 76th AVE.
WESTMINSTER, CO 80030

X

CH

DISCARD

THE COMPLETE MASTIFF

BETTY BAXTER
and DAVID BLAXTER

New York

WESTMINSTER PUBLIC LIBRARY
3031 WEST 76th AVE.
WESTMINSTER, CO 80030

Copyright © 1993 by Betty Baxter and David Blaxter

All rights reserved. No part of this book may be reproduced or transmitted in any form or by any means, electronic or mechanical, including photocopying, recording, or by any information storage and retrieval system, without permission in writing from the Publisher.

HOWELL BOOK HOUSE
A Simon & Schuster Macmillan company,
1633 Broadway, New York, NY 10019.

MACMILLAN is a registered trademark of Macmillan, Inc.

Library of Congress Cataloging-in-Publication data

Baxter, Betty.
    The complete mastiff / Betty Baxter and David Blaxter.

        p.   cm.
    ISBN 0-87605-234-0
    1. Mastiff.   I. Blaxter, David.   II. Title
    SF429.M36B37   1993   92-31093
    636.7'3 – dc20   CIP

10 9 8 7 6 5
Printed and bound in Singapore

CONTENTS

Chapter One: History of the Mastiff   5

Chapter Two: The Mastiff in North America   33

Chapter Three: The Mastiff in the Nineties   48

Chapter Four: Choosing a Puppy   59

Chapter Five: Training and Socialisation   67

Chapter Six: Caring for your Mastiff   74

Chapter Seven: The Breed Standard   83

Chapter Eight: The Show Ring   108

Chapter Nine: Breeding   116

Chapter Ten: Pregnancy and Whelping   127

Chapter Eleven: Rearing a Litter   135

Chapter Twelve: Health Care   147

Chapter Thirteen: Breed Clubs   158

*To Mastiffs through the
centuries and their breeders,
no matter who or where.*

ACKNOWLEDGEMENTS

We are most grateful to all those who supplied photographs. In particular we thank David Collinson, Cmdr Matthew Duke, Mary Joynes and Lyn Say.

Thanks also to those who supplied information about the Mastiff overseas, as well as photographs: Bob Silvaggi (USA), Diane Bearley (USA), and Andy Mayne for details of the Australian scene.

Finally, thanks to Sylvia Evans and Shirley Lambert for line drawings.

Chapter One

HISTORY OF THE MASTIFF

When tracing the origins of breeds of dogs, there is a tendency for every specialist to claim antiquity for their chosen breed, citing sculptures, writings and artefacts as evidence. However, the Mastiff is universally acknowledged as a very ancient breed. There were large, fierce dogs in Britain at the time of the Roman invasion, and Kingdom, writing in 1871, says that they were "indigenous to the country". Their size and courage ensured that they were exported to Rome for exhibition in the gladiatorial arenas, and, again according to Kingdom, and Wynn, an official was put in charge of their breeding and export.

Throughout all the ensuing years – through the times of the Romans, the Saxons and the Danes – Mastiffs, or dogs of that type, carried out the tasks for which they were bred: to guard the homesteads, the farms and the manor houses. They were guardians of property, not hunting dogs, although in the Middle Ages it was decreed that they should be 'lawed', i.e. that three toes of one front foot should be cut off to prevent them chasing the King's deer (Forest Laws, 1017). This big, fierce-looking English dog survived through the ages, and they were undoubtedly the original "dogs of war" mentioned by Shakespeare. In fact, Henry VIII apparently gave four-hundred Mastiffs to the King of France, Charles V, to be used as fighting dogs in battle.

Research points to the belief that the dogs mentioned in the Middle Ages, and before, were of a type, and not a breed as such, and were almost certainly not exactly like our Mastiffs of today; we have bred them much bigger over the last hundred years or so. But even so, they were bigger than any other canine, as indicated by written descriptions – "masteves be in alle the forests of England – of cherlich nature and foul shape" and "his head great; his eyes sharp and fierce; his countenance like a lion's, and large mightie bodie and a great shrill voice...". The Mastiff was most certainly a guard dog to be reckoned with.

From the Dark Ages, through Medieval and Tudor times, there were no pedigrees as such. Dogs were chosen for their ability to do their job, rather than for their looks. However, there is one exception, and this concerns the Lyme Hall Mastiffs. A Mastiff bitch belonging to Sir Piers Legh II, who was killed at Agincourt (1415), founded a strain of Mastiffs that only died out at Lyme Hall at the beginning of this century. We can see from pictures of these dogs that they were different from our Mastiffs of today, as their heads were narrower, their muzzles were more tapering, and the colours were different. Even so, looking at one, you would know that it was indeed a Mastiff. They were kept apart from other strains and were only bred at Lyme Hall. It is interesting to speculate whether the breed as we know it today would be exactly as it is now, if the Lyme Hall Mastiffs had been in existence and had been used in the resuscitation of the breed in the last century.

During the reign of Elizabeth I, Mastiffs were used in the terrible 'sport' of bull and bear baiting, but by the end of the 18th century the interest in these activities had declined (perhaps we have something to thank Oliver Cromwell for in the mid-seventeenth century, after all) and consequently the numbers of Mastiffs declined drastically. Whether it would be correct to say that the breed was almost extinct is difficult to say, but their numbers were certainly extremely low. There appeared to be very little call for these big dogs, although there were still dogs of the old type at various large country houses such as Chatsworth, Elvaston, and of course, Lyme Hall.

Looking back, some two hundred years later, it cannot be verified whether the breed was saved by chance or by design – whether a few gentlemen started to breed the 'pure' survivors to a plan, or whether it was an accident of fate. The ancestors of today's Mastiffs can be named as dogs of the very early 1800s, and the breeders that were were involved were: Commissioner Thompson of Halifax, Mr T. H. Lukey (the 'father of the modern Mastiff'), George White, the well-known dog dealer, and Sir George Armitage and his game-keeper, John Crabtree. This small nucleus gave the breed a starting point and something on which to build, and gradually the circle extended and interest increased. Commissioner Thompson's grandson, Mr J. W. Thompson, was actively breeding Mastiffs well into the latter part of the 19th century. T. Lukey acquired his first bitch from George White, and she was called Old Bob Tailed Countess. This bitch, together with another bitch called Duchess, found in a trap by John Crabtree, and Rose – the original bitch belonging to Thompson senior – would appear in all of today's pedigrees, if they were traced far

Mr Lukey's Mastiff, winner at the Leeds show in 1861.   The English Kennel Club.

enough back. By 1850 the breed was on a much sounder footing. There was some outcrossing to Alpines, as St Bernards were then called, and also probably to the Bulldog. This was the Regency Bulldog, and not the dog we know by that name today. This outcrossing was, no doubt, necessary because of the shortage of original stock, but it did lead to a lot of acrimonious correspondence in the following years when arguments about type, pedigrees and the outcrosses used, became extremely heated. However, despite the introduction of some alien blood, the dogs bred at this time were certainly the descendants of dogs that had been in Britain since time immemorial.

It is difficult to follow the fortunes of dogs in the first fifty years of the nineteenth century, because the same names were used over and over again. So you have 'Thompson's Duchess', 'Lukey's Governor', 'Lukey's Countess', and as these names occur with great frequency, you cannot always be one hundred per cent certain to which generation they refer! It is much easier to keep track of individual

A Mastiff (top, centre) in typical pose, owned by Mr Hindrey, featured in The Illustrated London News, 1861. Reproduced by kind permission of Kennel Gazette.

dogs and breeders after 1850, when records were better kept and there was much more interest in pedigrees, as such. By this date there was a far larger number of interested owners and breeders, and more information was available, if required by prospective owners.

THE GOLDEN ERA: 1850 to 1900
The second fifty years of the 19th century saw the rise and consolidation of the breed. In 1859 the very first dog show was held, and over the next decade such exhibitions became increasingly popular. The show at Crystal Palace held in 1872 attracted an entry of eighty-one Mastiffs, an enormous figure for any such event, and

the Old English Mastiff Club's first show, in 1890, had fifty-one entries. The OEMC had been formed in 1883, just ten years after the formation of the Kennel Club itself, and, of course, with the formation of the Kennel Club came the Stud Book, registrations, and the proper keeping of pedigrees.

Many more Mastiffs were being bred now, but there was one particular litter of note, born in 1867, and belonging to Miss Aglionby. It consisted of five dog puppies, and one of them, Turk, was to have a considerable influence on the breed. Again, he can be found in all our present-day pedigrees, and pictures of him show a dog which is undeniably a Mastiff, albeit with a slightly narrower muzzle than we like today. On the opposite side of the coin, we have Ch. Crown Prince, born in 1880. He had the kind of head which gave rise to great admiration and comment, and he was used extensively at stud. However, although his head was beautiful, he was almost a cripple, and he passed on this unsoundness to many of his offspring. Indeed, Mr W. K. Taunton, a very famous judge and breeder, writing over twenty-five years later, complained that "we are still suffering today", referring to the very weak hindquarters found in so many of the dogs of that time.

Despite this, there were many excellent Mastiffs being exhibited, and pictures of them show dogs that could win well in the ring today. Among these were Ch. Beaufort, Ch. Minting, Brampton Beauty, Cambrian Princess, Cardinal and Ch. Hotspur. The latter was a son of Crown Prince, but he seems to have escaped the terrible hindquarters of his father. The 1870s show an upsurge in numbers, but it appears to be the 1880s which gave a decade of general quality. Names of the breeders concerned include: Capt. Piddocke, Mr Beaufoy, Mr W. K. Taunton, Dr Sydney Turner, Mr Court Rice, Mr Hanbury, Mr Wigglesworth, and Betty Baxter's grandfather, Norman Higgs.

As previously mentioned, there was at this time, a good deal of acrimonious correspondence concerning the type of head and muzzle wanted, and the types of dogs that had been used in outcrossing. A certain James Watson always contended that the foundation stock used earlier was not pure-bred, but contained Great Dane blood and Alpine Mastiffs. Others argued equally fiercely that the strain was "pure" and "without taint of bull". It is quite impossible at this stage to know for sure, but obviously Alpine Mastiffs and Regency Bulldogs had been used to some extent out of sheer necessity; but, as already stated, it is quite certain that the Mastiff is the direct descendant of the original British dogs, even if their blood is somewhat diluted.

The other bone of contention in the 1880s and 1890s concerned, as always, the type of head and muzzle that was preferred. Leadbetter, a noted breeder, held that "a long-headed Mastiff is an abomination", as he maintained that "they are so much

Mr Leadbetter's Ch. Elgira, pictured in 1901. An example of the developing 'modern' type.

The English Kennel Club

easier to breed than the correct sort." In an article published in 1908 Sydney Turner wrote "there is a craze for abnormally short muzzles, which is a kind of obsession," and W. K. Taunton, called for a "medium in everything." Correspondence in those days was much more of the uncensored variety, and, indeed, more vitriolic than anything we encounter today. But even today, with type more stabilised than in the last century, there is, unfortunately, still a good deal of variation in heads, and a good deal of variation in the interpretation of the Breed Standard concerning them. Notwithstanding disagreements, excellent progress was made in these fifty years, and in many ways this era was one of the high points in the breed's existence.

THE BREED DECLINES: 1900-1920

The Mastiff, as a breed, has always been subject to fluctuations in popularity, and although the 1870s and 1880s were excellent years for the breed, by the end of the century the pendulum had swung the other way, and numbers were falling once more. In fact, in 1900 there were only three Challenge Certificates awarded, and the breed was once again at a low ebb. The situation improved very gradually over the next ten years, with forty-eight Mastiffs registered in 1906, and sixty registered in 1913. However, the war years of 1914-18 did enormous damage, with hardly any breeding taking place, and only three registrations were recorded in 1918.

It was during the early years of the 1900s that the first mention is made of registrations for 'Bull and Mastiffs,' at the Kennel Club, and these crossbreeds were, for one reason or another, used quite extensively in the breeding programme of Mastiff breeders in the post-war years. This is surprising in view of the fact that there were still pure-bred Mastiffs available, but nevertheless, these outcrosses appear very frequently in Mastiff pedigrees of the 1920s – to the fury of the committee of the Old English Mastiff Club. However, it has to be remembered that the Bull Mastiff owed its existence to the Mastiff in the first place, and it is amusing to see the Kennel Club records of that time showing Mastiff dogs with Bullmastiff blood in their veins being used to produce 'registered' progeny of both Mastiffs and Bull and Mastiffs.

In the First World War Mastiffs were used for pulling gun carriages and ammunition carts. This Mastiff is pictured with two soldiers in Belgium.

THE FIRST REVIVAL: 1920 to 1940
The 1920s was the start of a period of growth, stability and authority, despite the previous disagreements between breeders and the blow dealt by the war. This decade saw the emergence of three major kennels, and two of these continued to be of influence until well after the Second World War. The three were Mr and Mrs Scheerboom's Havengore Mastiffs, Miss Bell and her Withybush line (although the prefix was not actually registered until after the Second World War), and Mr and Mrs Oliver, owners of the Hellingly kennels. The Scheerbooms and Miss Bell used the lines carrying the Bull and Mastiff blood, while the Olivers opposed these most strongly, and refused to have anything to do with the lines 'tainted' in this way.

The committee of the OEMC condemned the use of 'mixed' breeding stock wholeheartedly. However, it is amusing to note that the Scheerbooms, whose famous Ch. Bill of Havengore, with his superb head, carried so much of this blood, and Miss

A typical Mastiff of the type produced before the Second World War.

Bell, whose Woden was likewise part Bull and Mastiff, were members of the OEMC and were, in fact, on the judging list, whereas the Olivers kept themselves slightly apart. From the surviving photographs, it appears that the Hellingly dogs were of good type, but with slightly longer muzzles than the Havengores. Their foundation stud dog was Ch. Joseph of Hellingly. Judging from hearsay, there was little love lost between the Havengores and the Hellinglys. It is to Miss Bell that we owe the continuation of the lovely brindle colour, as, apart from Ch. Marksman of Hellingly, brindles were extremely rare. However, Miss Bell had more brindles than the other kennels, and her Lady Turk was a most beautiful brindle bitch.

Some breeders from pre-war days were still active, such as George Cook and his son, Mr H. Cook, with their Cleveland Mastiffs, Mr Hunter Johnson, Guy Greenwood, and Mr W. K. Taunton, who was still judging, but there were also several newcomers. Some of the best-known of these were: Mr R. Thomas (Menai), Mrs Edgar (Delevals), Mr L. Crook (Tiddicars), and the very well-known Broomcourt dogs, who were owned by Mr B. Bennett. It would be quite difficult to mention all the kennels of this period, as the breed was increasing both in numbers and in stature.

By the 1930s the 'new' blood had been assimilated, and it was not causing so much debate and acrimony – although the Hellinglys were still avoiding any contact with it like the plague. Whether this assimilation was a good thing or not is immaterial; it was there, it had happened, and, as previously stated, Bull and Mastiffs were descended from Mastiffs in the first place. The breed notes, printed in

Mrs Oliver and her Hellingly Mastiffs.

Fall.

Ch. Joy of Hellingly (Ch. Joseph of Hellingly – Ch. Joy of Wantley), born February 1929.

the weekly dog papers, were still full of sound and fury concerning the prevalence of such outcrossing, and much of what was printed would not be allowed to appear in today's papers but they certainly make very interesting reading! Differing head types, with reference to the Breed Standard, were still a cause of debate – and we can only speculate as to why Mastiffs, who are normally such peaceable dogs, should provoke fury on the part of their owners.

Registrations in the 1930s increased noticeably, with 164 in 1933. The most notable occurrence of the 1930s was the disbandment of the Hellingly kennels. Tragedy struck the Olivers and almost overnight all the dogs were dispersed. Most of them were sent to the United States, and it is these Hellingly dogs that provide the foundation for the stock that was returned to Britain after the war. This loss of an influential and powerful kennel was a great blow to the breed in general, which was made even more severe by the outbreak of war in 1939. Many Mastiffs were sent to America, but many more were destroyed, and breeding came almost completely to a halt.

THE BREED BORDERS ON EXTINCTION: 1940-1950
There were just three litters bred during the war years. A bitch called Hortia was owned by a Mrs Park, and she was of Deleval breeding. When she was mated to Ch. Christopher of Havengore she produced a litter on December 5th 1939. One of these puppies was Robin of Brunwins, and on the October 8th 1943, Hortia produced a litter to her son, Robin. One of these puppies was Sally of Coldblow, and it is to this one bitch that we owe the single uninterrupted English bloodline, as she was the only Mastiff of breeding age left at the end of the war. Hortia produced a third litter, also to Robin, when she was seven years old. This was in 1944, but there is no trace of the resulting litter producing progeny, so it was left to Sally to secure the breed's salvation.

There was also a brindle dog, which had been parted from its owner by the blitz. The story is quite well-known, but to this day it cannot be said with any degree of certainty whether the dog was a Mastiff, a Bullmastiff, or a cross between the two. The Kennel Club registered him as Templecombe Torus, a Mastiff, and it was this dog that was mated to Sally. She produced a litter in 1947 which contained Nydia of Frithend. She was the only bitch – and the only member of the litter to be bred from – so through Sally, and then her daughter Nydia, the tenuous thread of succession continued. There has, to date, been no record found of Torus producing any other stock.

It was patently obvious that fresh blood was urgently needed, especially as any other male Mastiff which had survived the war was far too old to sire puppies. Mrs Heather Mellhuish, of British Columbia, eventually sent over a pair of Canadian-bred puppies. They were very closely related, but they were still a godsend: they were Heatherbelle Stirling Silver and Heatherbelle Portia (later registered a Heatherbelle Portia of Goring). One other import arrived in 1947, and that was Jana of Mansatta, who was brought in and registered by a Mr Bowles. She was a welcome addition, but she was not as prolific as Nydia and Portia. Portia went to live with Miss Bell, and Silver went to Mrs Scheerboom. Their pedigrees go back through Mrs Mellhuish's kennels, to those of Merle Cambell and the dogs exported to the United States in the early part of the 1930s.

Another extremely important American import was the brindle Valiant Diadem,

Heatherbelle Bearehills Rajah (right) and Heatherbelle Bearehill Priscilla's Amelia.

Heatherbelle Bearehills Priscilla's Amelia with A. W. Duke.

Heatherbelle Bearehills Rajah and Heatherbelle Bearehills Priscilla's Amelia with one of their offspring, probably Abigail.

obtained from Robert Burns, and descended from Hellingly dogs. He was mated to Nydia and to Portia, and from 1949 onwards, puppies started to appear. They were registered with the prefix 'OEMC' as the Kennel Club, in this single instance, allowed a breed club to register its own prefix. Two more Heatherbelle puppies were imported privately in 1949 – Heatherbelle Bearehills Rajah and Heatherbelle Bearehills Priscillas Amelia. It is not thought that Amelia produced registered stock, but Rajah did a certain amount of stud work. Heatherbelle Priscilla's Martha was imported by Dr and Mrs Mayne, and she was the foundation of their Fanifold kennels.

Pedigree of Heatherbelle Sterling Silver and Heatherbelle Portia, born 1947. (From imported American stock).

King Rufus Of Parkhurst	**Emblem Of Parkhurst**	Alters Big Jumbo	Buster Of Saxondale / Angeles Victoria
		Manthorne Joy	Buddy / Millfold Lass
	Joy Of Parkhurst	Alters Big Jumbo	Buster Of Saxondale / Angeles Victoria
		Manthorne Joy	Buddy / Millfold Lass
Heatherbelle Lady Hyacinth	**Shanno Of Lyme Hall**	Angeles Tristram	Brian Of Roxbroom / Goldhawk Elsie
		Merles Brunhilde Of Lyme Hall	Roxbury Boy / Buzzard Pride
	Merles Tanna	Faxon Of Altnacraig	Boyce Of Altnacraig / Maud Of Hellingly
		Angeles Empress	Angeles King / Rolanda

Therefore, at the end of the 1940s there was a situation where all the Mastiff stock consisted of the Heatherbelle dogs, Jana, Valiant Diadem, and Nydia. It is obvious that with such a tiny number of Mastiffs a tremendous amount of in-breeding had to take place. The pedigrees of that time are quite amazing, and they stamped the type on the breed for generations, for both good and bad points. Heads were usually very good, but soundness was sometimes suspect.

Even with the puppies such as OEMC Prudence, OEMC Countess, OEMC Boadicea, OEMC Baroness, and others, the position was still not really safe, although at that time we had started to export the occasional Mastiff back to the United States, such as Withybush Magnus, bred by Miss Bell. He was sired by Stirling out of Prudence, who was a Diadem/Nydia daughter. In the United States he was mated to a Peach Farm bitch and a resulting son, Weyacres Lincoln, was sent

Ch. Threebees Friar of Copenore (Jason of Copenore – Cleopatra of Saxondale), a highly influential sire.

back to Britain in 1952. This dog still appears on the edge of some of today's pedigrees, among the older animals, and he appeared to have been mated to just about every Mastiff bitch capable of breeding – after all, he offered the only tiny bit of fresh blood. Lincoln, his son, Jason of Copenore, and grandson, Threebees Friar of Copenore, were three outstanding and most influential stud dogs of the fifties and sixties.

Miss Bell, pictured in 1957, with Withybush Froda and Withybush Fausta, seven-month-old daughters of Ch. Withybush Aethelred out of Withybush Bess.

THE BREED CONSOLIDATES: 1950-1970

During the fifties numbers crept up again, and the breed was firmly re-established. Mrs Scheerboom and the Havengores produced the majority of show winners, and the very first post-war Champion was Ch. Rodney of Havengore. The first bitch to be made up after the war was OEMC Countess. Both Mrs Scheerboom and Miss Bell were the pre-eminent breeders at this time, but gradually the circle increased. Mrs Day started her Hollesley kennels, with Ch. Dawn of Havengore as her foundation bitch; Mrs Harrild owned the Moonsfield kennels, and Mr and Mrs Lindley formed the Copenore kennels – they owned the famous Jason, and bred Friar. Mr and Mrs Taylor's Saxondale kennels were founded in the early 1930s, and they recommenced breeding at this time, and Mr, Mrs and Miss Perrenoud's small but elite Meps dogs were always to the fore. Another well-known name was Kisumu, the prefix belonging to Rene Creigh.

Registrations increased in the immediate post war-years: 49 in 1953 rising to 58 in 1959, and in 1960 this went up to 99. All the signs were encouraging at last, with more dogs, more breeders, and far more interest in the breed among the general public.

A beautiful fawn Mastiff, typical of the type produced in the fifties.

The OEMC's first post-war Championship Show at Pangbourne Nautical College, with an entry of fifty-seven Mastiffs judged by Mrs N. Dicken. Pictured (left to right) are Mrs Willis with Cherry of Havengore, Mrs Lewis with Bardayle Storma of Stoan, Mr W. Hanson with Gypsy of Havengore, Mrs P. Day with Ch. Dawn of Havengore and Mrs L. Scheerboom with Louise of Havengore.

*A group of
Havengore
Mastiffs.*

Ch. Balint of Havengore, sired by Ch. Hotspot of Havengore.

Early in the 1960s, the death of Miss Bell shook the Mastiff world. This lady had been active in the breed since 1924, and had played a major part in helping to save it after the war. It seemed inconceivable that she was no longer involved with the breed. Added to the loss of Miss Bell herself, was the further blow of her last instructions for all her dogs to be put down. She obviously meant this for the best, but with breeding stock still not truly numerous, it was a severe setback for the breed as a whole. A few of her dogs were spared – one bitch nursing a litter, Withybush Superbus, Withybush Etta, and one other bitch. These were found pet homes, and the prefix Withybush will always be remembered. There were some very fine dogs bred by Mrs Scheerboom in the late 1950s and throughout the early 1960s. They seemed unbeatable, and Betty can remember the impression that they left on her when she saw them at shows. They included: Ch. Drake of Havengore, Ch. Hotspot of Havengore, Ch. Diana of Havengore, Hugh of Havengore, Cathie of Havengore, Ch. Balint of Havengore – the list is almost endless. Betty has a particularly soft spot for the gorgeous apricot dog, Balint, as she took her foundation bitch to him and the Farnaby kennels are therefore founded, in part, on the Havengore line. New kennels which started in the 1960s included the well-known Buckhalls, owned by Major and Mrs Reardon (they bought in Friar of Copenore); Mr Cogan began his Craigavon strain; Mrs Day increased her dogs, and among these was the truly beautiful Ch. Macushla of Hollesley; Dr Allison, who lived in Yorkshire, had the Weatherhill Mastiffs and she bred Ch. Thor and Bellringer from her lovely big, fawn bitch, Ch. Weatherhill Milf Manetta. These were days full of promise and hope, with good dogs and breeders doing their best to produce excellent stock. The Lindleys continued to breed and show their Copenore Mastiffs, with Jason and Friar shining as the foremost stud dogs, even when up against the Havengores.

THE PRESENT-DAY MASTIFF

The 1970s continued the upward trend, and this was a time of expansion. Registrations for 1971 rose to 154 and by 1978 reached 279, recording the highest ever, 316, for 1980. Many new kennels started in the breed, they include the Bulliffs, which was founded in 1970 when Mrs Say bought President of Shute, a Threebees-Friar son, and this remains an influential kennel today. Mrs Robson-Jones and the Gildasan Mastiffs started in the early 1970s, and remain a force to be reckoned with. The Hicks family founding their Jilgrajons kennels, Vivian Corbett (Jakotes) and Sylvia Shorter (Canonbury) all made important contributions. Some of these are no longer active, through ill health or other reasons, but many who began in Mastiffs at that time are well-known names today, and have lost none of their interest and enthusiasm.

President of Shute: sire of five English Champions and foundation of the Bulliff Kennel.

Ch. Bulliff Warrior: twice Best of Breed at Crufts.

Bulliff Razzermataz.

Bulliff Zeb, who worked as a PAT (Therapy) dog.

Ch. Jilgrajon Sir Gladstone (Ch. Cemaes King Edward of Jilgrajon – Ch. Jilgrajon Lady Victoria). Mastiff of the Year, 1980 and winner of nine CCs and five RCCs.

Ch. Hollesley Medicine Man: best of
Breed at Crufts on four different
occasions in the eighties.
Pearce.

A very interesting kennel of the 1970s and early 1980s was that of Mrs Degerdon, and the Grangemoor Mastiffs. Although she is no longer part of the Mastiff scene now, she did own some very beautiful dogs, including Ch. Copenore Rab, Ch. Hollesley Machushlas Dagda, Ch. Copenore Czarina and Ch. Grangemoor Bevis. One of the all-time greats was Ch. Dare Devil of Hollesley, a superb fawn dog, who was owned by Mrs Degerdon. She appeared to buy in more than she bred, but Rab sired the famous Ch. Hollesley Medicine Man, who in his day was almost unbeatable and was Best of Breed at Crufts on four occasions in the early 1980s.

Throughout the years, America has imported Mastiffs from Britain, and relatively few have been taken in exchange, but a dog arrived in the 1970s that was to make an impact on the breed. This was Ch. The Devil from Wayside, imported by Vivien Corbett, and later bought by Mrs Degerdon. He was a distant descendant of the Dogue de Bordeaux, Fenelle de Fenelon, owned by Merle Cambell, and proved to be

Am. Eng. Ch. Arcinegas Lion of Bredwardine: an important sire whose offspring have made a great mark on the breed as it enters the nineties.
Pearce.

a good dog for the breed, producing some excellent stock, although the legacy he bequeathed as far as head type and pigment was concerned, left something to be desired.

The upward trend in the breed continued into the 1980s, and many of these kennels are still active today in the early 1990s. Names which will be familiar to today's Mastiff owners are Messrs Thomas and Tugwell and their Bredwardine kennel. In fact the kennels were founded in the mid 1970s with a Farnaby bitch, Farnaby Voodoo Princess, but in the last ten years they have grown so much in

Ch. Bredwardine Brongest, litter brother of 'Bedwyr', son of 'Lion'.   *Pearce.*

stature and in importance – they are probably the largest Mastiff kennels in the UK at the present time. In 1985 they imported the American and English Champion Arcinegas Lion of Bredwardine. This dog has had a great influence on the breed, and the progeny that he sired – and he sired many – are in many instances better than he, and this is the mark of a good stud. Lion was a big apricot, and his sons and daughters, and his grandchildren, are all winning well in the ring today. He was one of the most successful of imports, and his death at a comparatively early age was a very sad loss.

Ch. Bredwardine Bedwyr, a quality son of 'Lion'.   *Pearce.*

Raymond Boatwright founded his Glynpedr line, another very famous establishment, in the early 1980s; Mr and Mrs Sargeant (Trevabyn), Mr and Mrs Joynes (Damarias), Ann Davies (Nantymyndd – founded in the 60s) were all going strong in the 1980s, as was Betty's Farnaby line. A number of today's successful kennels were founded on Farnaby and Lesdon stock – Lesdon is Betty's husband's prefix – and this is a source of pride and satisfaction. In fact, David (Blaxter) started his Namous kennels with a Lesdon bitch – the beautiful Int. Ch. Lesdon Lady Betteresse. David's Ch. Uberacht of Namous, a big brindle dog, won very well in the

Ch. Chevelu Blodeuwedd of Bredwardine, sired by 'Lion' out of Cedwalla English Rose of Chevelu, bred by Meg Duval.   *Pearce.*

late 1980s, going Best of Breed at Crufts on more than one occasion. The Namous line (and Sylvia Blaxter's Masnou line also), like the Bredwardine, is one of the larger and more influential of kennels.

As new kennels have emerged, some of the old names have disappeared. Mrs Scheerboom died at the very end of the 1970s, and with her death came the end of an era. The Havengores had dominated the Mastiff scene since the early 1920s and will always be remembered with respect. All Mastiff owners owe the Havengores a great deal, and it is to be hoped that we can continue to breed the type of Mastiffs

Ch. Bredwardine Beau Ideal, a daughter of Farnaby Voodoo Princess. Beau Ideal was Mastiff Of The Year 1983, Mastiff Bitch of the Year 1985, holder of bitch CC record.

Pearce.

she strived for. Major Reardon of the Buckhall Mastiffs, and Rene Creigh of the Kisumus, both died in the early 1980s; Sylvia Shorter and the Canonburys emigrated to South Africa, and unhappily the Sargeants with the Trevabyns have also retired from the Mastiff scene. A decade of change, but hopefully too of fresh interest, and with new enthusiasts.

Registrations continue to increase, despite the difficulties of recession, and there is no evidence of entries at shows decreasing either. Mastiffs today are not kept in large kennels, with a few exceptions, but are mostly kept in ones or twos, and

Ch. Zanfi
Princess Tanya of
Damaria.

Orlando, a
brother of Ch.
Zanfi Princess
Tanya of
Damaria.

Damaria Indian Chief (Ch. Damaria Count Magnum – Ch. Zanfi Princess Tanya of Damaria).

Ch. Damaria Count Magnum, aged eight months.

Glynpedr Harvey Warbanger of Namous, a typical Glynpedr dog, grandson of Ch. Hollesley Medicine Man.

Ch. Uberacht of Namous (Ch. Ramuncho des Verts Tilleuls and Lesdon Lady Betteresse of Namous): Crufts Best of Breed winner in 1988 and 1989, pictured in his prime at six years of age.

mainly as house pets. This certainly suits their temperaments and characters, as this breed blossoms in human company. The majority of kennels that are active in the breed are not run as large, commercial establishments. They are generally quite small in size, with comparatively few dogs – although these are top quality – and the Mastiff, bred to be guardians of the home and family, thrives in this environment.

Chapter Two

THE MASTIFF IN NORTH AMERICA

THE FIRST MASTIFFS

The history of the Mastiff in America and Canada is bound up inextricably with the United Kingdom. It is a matter of question as to whether there were Mastiffs in the New World in the 18th century, although they are mentioned in writings, but these would probably be unlike the breed as we know it – large heavy dogs, but differing from today's Mastiffs.

In the late 1800s, with the breed flourishing in its home country, interest likewise increased in America. Dr David Collinson, in an interesting article, states that Captain Garner brought in two Mastiffs, Adam and Eve, in 1857. In the latter part of the 19th century numbers increased dramatically, with a steady cross-Atlantic passage of dogs in both directions. (There was no UK quarantine in those days.) This was also the start of dog shows as we know them today, on both sides of the ocean.

Registrations soared during the last twenty years of the 19th century, but for some inexplicable reason they fell away to almost nothing in the next decade, with only one being shown in the registrations for 1909, one for 1910, one for 1911 and none for 1912. It would seem likely that the pre First World War bloodlines died out and the breed started afresh with imports to Canada in 1918 and the early 1920s.

THE WINGFIELD KENNELS

The story of C. W. Dickinson, of Toronto, who owned a dog called Beowulf, is intriguing, although it is difficult to find out very much about either dog or man. Dickinson was the owner and founder of the Canadian Wingfield kennels, and during the latter part of the First World War he imported Priam of Wingfield and Parkgate Duchess. Both these animals were of pure English breeding, but whether they were imported from England, or whether their parents were imported, is not clear. According to Mrs P. Hoffman, an authority on American registrations, these two were the parents of Beowulf. These were the basis of the Wingfield kennels. To say they were inbred is an understatement, because if pedigrees are correct, they show that Conrad of Wingfield and Boadicea of Wingfield, both by Priam out of Duchess, produced a dog called Wodan the Saxon. This dog, a product of a full brother-sister mating, was then mated to Princess Mary, herself a daughter to Priam and Parkgate Duchess. Perhaps with the dearth of Mastiffs in Canada and the United States at that time, there was nothing else to be done.

These early Canadian pedigrees certainly make most interesting reading. Princess Mary and Wodan produced Mary of Knollwood, and she, mated to Beowulf, managed to produce some fresh bloodlines. At a later date she was mated to Welend, who had been exported to Canada in 1924. This kennel kept the breed going in North America, and, through one of their descendants, contributes to the bloodlines of every Mastiff alive today. This is because Priam and Duchess's great-grand-daughter Betty is the bitch behind Patty Brill's famous Peach Farm Kennels. Dickinson died in 1928, the year before the Mastiff Club of America was formed, but he and the Wingfields had ensured that the breed would survive in America. It is strange, but almost immediately after he died there was an upsurge of interest in the breed and importations from Britain started again. However, there appears to be a break in the USA between dogs bred prior to the 1914-1918 war and those of the 1930s and 1940s, with the exception, of course, of the Canadian Wingfields.

THE BREED DEVELOPS

One of the most prolific importers of Mastiffs in the 1930s was Percy Hobart Titus, who brought in from England the litter brother and sister Roxbury Boy and Millfold Lass, together with Goldhawk Elsie. His prefix was Manthorpe, and a glance at American pedigrees of this time will show that he was very active. Titus also imported Buzzard Pride from Ireland, and Broomcourt Nell and Rolanda from the UK, in 1936 and 1940 respectively. His kennels are also behind Harry Veach's Angeles Mastiffs, Merle Cambell's kennels, and Patty Brill's Peach Farm kennels. Merle Cambell's dogs – Merles Tanna, Shanno of Lyme Hall and Merles Brunhilde of Lyme Hall – are, in turn, of importance because they provided the foundation stock for the Canadian Heatherbelles, owned by Heather Mellhuish.

Another famous kennel of the 1930s, immediately pre-war and through the 1940s, was the Altnacraigs, owned by James Foster Clark. They benefited enormously from the break-up of the renowned Hellingly kennels in England, and Foster Clark brought in King, Maud, Duke, Kathleen, Katrina and Monarch of Hellingly, as well as Gyn of Hammercliffe. Some of these dogs were sent to America for safety's sake because of the war, but the majority came because of the demise of the Hellinglys. These Hellingly/Altnacraig dogs also provided the foundation for the Leitchs' Knockrivochs and the Fricks' Mansattas – two other important American lines.

Patty Brill's famous Peach Farm kennels was based on British dogs imported by Titus, and also through the one single line it goes back to Betty, a Canadian descendant of the Wingfields. Peach Farm can therefore lay claim to having the only unbroken line in North America, back to pre-First World War Mastiffs. All the other kennels were founded in the the late 1920s and 1930s. Peach Farm spanned almost five decades, from 1935, and was deservedly world famous.

NORTH AMERICA TO THE RESCUE
Britain suffered during the Second World War and Mastiffs nearly became extinct, but breeders in North America benefited because many were sent there for safety. This was to prove the salvation of the breed in Britain, because descendants of those dogs sent to the United States, were re-imported to the UK in 1947 and 1948, and helped save the breed in its native country. This rescue was brought about chiefly by the importation of four Heatherbelle puppies from Mrs Mellhuish in Canada; Valiant Diadem purchased from Robert Burn; and Craig and Sheba of Mansatta. These Mastiffs came to England in 1947 and 1948, and a look at their pedigrees shows how they all came from famous American lines which had been based on British stock, therefore preserving continuity, pre and post-war.

One other crucial importation was that of Weyacres Lincoln, sent to Britain in 1952 by Mrs Weyenburg. Lincoln was a son of Withybush Magnus (himself a son of one of the Canadian imports, with his mother being a Valiant Diadem daughter), who had been sent to America. He was mated to one of Patty Brill's Peach Farm bitches, Peach Farm Priscilla, and the resultant Lincoln brought some desperately needed fresh blood to the UK. The help which American and Canadian Mastiff owners gave their British counterparts ensured that the breed recovered in Britain; it is doubtful whether it could have survived without this aid. Despite the very low numbers of Mastiffs in England in the 1950s, it is surprising to see that even then, some dogs were being exported to America – Ch. Beowulf and Ch. Twinkle of Havengore and Copenore Libra among them.

LEADING BREEDERS
By the late 1950s in the United States, the Altnacraigs, Mansattas, Knockrivochs

Pedigree of Valiant Diadem, Born 30-6-1948.

Hector Of Knockrivoch	Eric Of Altnacraig	King Of Hellingly	King Baldur of Hellingly / Elaine Of Hellingly
		Maud Of Hellingly	Ch. Marksman Of Hellingly / Girl Of Trelyon
	Gyn Of Hammercliffe	Ch. Christopher Of Havengore	Mark Of Havengore / Diana Of Havengore
		Prunella (Exp USA 1940)	Ch. Uther Penavon / Hermia
Valiant Cythera	Alters Big Jumbo	Buster Of Saxondale	Brutus Of Saxondale / Dorothy W
		Angeles Victoria	Griffins Boss / Angeles Queen
	Olivia Of Mansatta	Gail Of Altnacraig	Aldwin Of Altnacraig / Kathleen Of Hellingly
		Blythe Of Hampden	Crusader Of Goring / Blythe Of Altnacraig

Pedigree of Weyacres Lincoln, born 1952.

Withybush Magnus	Heatherbelle Sterling Silver	King Rufus Of Parkhurst	Emblem Of Parkhurst / Joy Of Parkhurst
		Heatherbelle Lady Hyacinth	Shanno Of Lyme Hall / Merles Tanna
	OEMC Prudence	Valiant Diadem	Hector Of Knockrivoch / Valiant Cythera
		Nydia Of Frithend	Templecombe Taurus / Sally Of Coldblow
Peach Farm Priscilla	Austin Of Chaseways	Angeles President	Angeles King Of Altnacraig / Rolanda
		Gwendoline Of Altnacraig	Aldwin Of Altnacraig / Kathleen Of Hellingly
	Peach Farm Belinda	Hector Of Knockrivoch	Eric Of Altnacraig / Gyn Of Hammercliffe
		Peach Farm Rosita	Manthorne Mogul / Peach Farm Hugonette

Betty (second from left) presents Doona Balham's Old Schools Ursa Major with Best of Breed at the Mastiff Championship Show, Memphis, 1983.

Ch. Old Schools Lady Jillian: Best of Winners and Best Opposite Sex, Bucks County, 1992, judged by Mary Joynes.

Am. Ch. Damaria The Druid, pictured at twenty months.

Diane and William Bearley's Glyndwr Mastiffs: Ch. Glyndwr Gwilym and Ch. Glyndwr Sidonwy (Ch. Damaria The Druid – Ch. Tamarack Ernestine), pictured at thirteen months.   *Callea Photo.*

and Angeles kennels had all vanished from the scene. To counter these losses, other kennels came into being, among them the Weyacres, the Moorleigh kennels, owned by Marie Moore, the Boltes' Reveille kennels (the latter still active today), and the Olsens, with their Willowledge dogs. Merle Cambell and Patty Brill were still active; the breed was spreading and increasing, registrations were improving and the whole scene looked set fair.

An important event took place in 1959 when Merle Cambell registered the Dogue de Bordeaux, Fenelle de Fenelon, as a Mastiff and inbred on her to a surprising degree. A Dogue de Bordeaux has many attributes at variance with the Mastiff and although it certainly brought in fresh blood, and had an enormous influence on the breed, whether this is good or bad is a matter of opinion.

During the 1960s, 1970s and 1980s, the popularity of the breed in the United States has increased out of all recognition, with registrations going from around 200 in 1970 to 1500 and more in the 1980s. There have, of course, also been losses and in many ways the 1980s have been a sad time for Mastiffs in America. Merle Cambell, Marie Moore and Patty Brill have all died, leaving an enormous gap, and

Am. Ch. Oranshore Brutus Britt, imported into Britain by E. Waterhouse.

Eve Olsen and her Willowledge dogs have retired from the scene. There are now only a very few breeders still involved in the breed who were active in the post-war era – Damara Bolte and her Reveille kennel being one of them.

However, there are certainly far more Mastiffs in North America than anywhere else in the world, spread over a vast area. This very vastness brings its own problems, and there can be quite apparent regional differences. With the thousands of miles that have to be travelled for show or stud, it is perhaps only logical that breeders should tend to occur and remain in pockets, so dogs in Florida may differ slightly from those in New Jersey, California or the Mid West. Registrations of Mastiffs in the United States were 2,247 in 1989, 2,712 in 1990 and 2,886 in 1991.

The parent club is the Mastiff Club of America and entries in its Specialties run into hundreds. There are a number of regional Mastiff clubs, which are individually

Robert Silvaggi's Mistletoe Desert Storm (Ch. L. Olympus Zeus – Ch. Mistletoe Rev It Up).

Ch. Bankhouse Baccara (Ch. Gildsan Roman Warrior – Winterwood Eglantine).   Bernard W. Kernan.

*Ch. Iron Hills
Rocky Hill Thor.*

*Ch. Falmorehall
Mistral of Deer
Run, a daughter of
Farnaby Fighting
Faith of
Falmorehall.*

formed and named, and these may or may not become affiliated to the BCOA. Entries at these shows vary considerably from location to location. Betty had the honour of judging the very first Independent Specialty, in 1983, and the entry reached almost 200, taking the entries in the Stakes classes into account.

America has many excellent kennels, and although it would be impossible to mention them all, a selection would include: the Tamarack Mastiffs, belonging to Carole Knutson, and the Gulph Mills of the Gensburgers, both well established and well-known on the West Coast. The Strongs' Windor kennels, also of California, do not seem to be active at the moment. Across to the East, there are the Deer Run Mastiffs belonging to Tobin Jackson, and, of course, the Lazy Hill and Storm Mastiffs belonging to Virginia Bregman and Dee Dee Andersson. Coming down to

Tobin Jackson with Am. Ch. Deer Run Wyecliffe, a top sire who has made a great contribution to American Mastiffs.

West Virginia, we find Lynn Urban's Lyndons, and the Old School kennels of John and Donna Bahlman. Betty made one of the Old School bitches Best of Breed in the 1983 Specialty, and reckons that Old Schools Ursa Major had one of the best heads that she has ever seen. Scott Phoebus and his well-known Iron Hills dogs are always a force to be reckoned with. They are always presented in immaculate condition.

MASTIFF KENNELS IN THE UNITED STATES THAT ARE CURRENTLY BREEDING AND/OR EXHIBITING INCLUDE:

Agincourt Mastiffs	J. & V. Modica	Country Creek	Elizabeth & Fred Simon
Altom's	Alma Bowman	Deer Run	Tobin Jackson
Apple Creek	Terry Theriault	Diablo Mastiffs	S. & C. Medinas
Applewhaites Farm	Laura Sullivan	Dogwood Knoll	J. & P. Spears
Avalon Mastiffs	Catherine Angus	Double Edge Kennels	Susan & Terry Swords
Banyon Kennels	Mary Zellen	Durham Mastiffs	Deborah Barrioz
Bell Hollow Kennels	Hilary & Carl Tunick	Eldorado Mastiffs	Holly & Boyd Coller
Black Point Kennels	Diane Collings	Foxglove Mastiffs	Laura & David Hagey
Blacknight	LaVelle Knight	Gelwil Farms	Joanne Williams
Blue Ridge	Susan & Sheldon Giventer	Glyndwr Mastiffs	Diane & William Bearley
Brite Star Mastiffs	B. & L. House	Greco Mastiffs	Mrs Frank Greco
Burns-Hall Mastiffs	Bobby Burns	Greiner Hall	Steven Napotnik
Caledonia	Susanne Farber	Groppetti Mastiffs	P. Groppetti

Gulph Mills	Dee & Mike Gensburger	Northwood	Darrell Sather
Hale	Marge & Henry Levine	Old School	Donna Bahlman
His Majesty's Mastiffs	Eva Gomez	Pax River Mastiffs	Karl Greve
Horcado Ranch	Mary Lattimore	Pendragon Mastiffs	Susan & Bill Krauser
Iron Hills	Scott Phoebus	Petrosec/Big Bend	Ruth & William Brady
Ironlion Mastiffs	Jamie Klatsky	Pinehollow Mastiffs	Nancy & William Hempel
Jai-Bee	Irene Byrne	Quail Hill Mastiffs	Gigi Bacon
Knightsen Mastiffs	S. & R. Yurkovick	Rydalmount	Charles Cuthbert
L. Olympus Mastiffs	Shirley & Fred Camett	Sidetrack Farm	Jane Landis
Lazy Hill	Virginia Bregman	Sillars Mastiffs	Jeb Sillar
Legendary	Jeanne Cook	Smok'n Lad Mastiffs	Marianne Jackson
Lion Hearted	Gloria Davis	Southport Mastiffs	Joe Sanchez
Lyndon Mastiffs	Lynn Urban	Stablemate Mastiffs	Cynthia Campbell
Magnolia	Laurie Brooke Adams	Stonehouse Mastiffs	Karen & Michael McBee
Mastiffs of Albion	Jason Wasserman	Storm Mastiffs	Dee Dee & Bjorn Andersson
Mastiffs of Goldleaf	Robert Goldblatt	Tamarack Mastiffs	Carole Smith
Meriwether Mastiffs	E. & R. Montgomery	Tejas Mastiffs	Edward Ludwig
Mistletoe	Robert & Rebecca Silvaggi	The Abbey	Elizabeth Dickey
Night Stalker Kennel	Richard Cisneros	Villa Sturla Mastiffs	G. Sturla
Noble Hall Mastiffs	Anne Amadon	Windy Hill Mastiffs	Susan & Frank Routa

CANADA

Mr C. W. Dickinson of Toronto and his Wingfield kennels supplied the United States with Mastiffs from 1918 onwards, and so Canada played a very important part in the history of the breed. Dickinson obtained his original stock from England, although his kennels did become very inbred. He owned Beowulf, a well-known dog who did a lot of winning at that time. Beowulf was sold in 1917 to Dickinson's friend and partner, Mr W. O. Ingle of New York, but continued to be used at stud on his previous owner's bitches. Dickinson and Ingle remained in collaboration until Dickinson's death in 1928. So it can be said that the early 1920s were a period of quite considerable activity for the breed in Canada, spilling over into the northern part of the United States.

It is interesting to note that a Mastiff Club was started in Toronto seven years before the inception of the present Mastiff Club of America, in 1929. Mr Dickinson was the president, with Mr Ingle doubling as both treasurer and secretary. However, the club was very short-lived, and none of its records have survived. The last Mastiff bred at the Wingfield kennels appears to have been Betty, who was sold to a Mr Beer in the United States, in 1929.

The last recorded import from England into Canada was made in 1930 with Thor of the Isles, whelped on the December 25th 1926. This dog was very inbred and carried a great deal of Bull and Mastiff blood. In fact, this bloodline was introduced into North America through this animal. Thor, in his turn, was sold to Mr. Beer, and

*Kay
Langshaw
with one of
her Solstice
Mastiffs.*

was mated to Betty. Their daughters, Maizie of St Paul and Bayberry June are six generations behind Valiant Diadem (imported into England immediately post-war) and seven generations behind Weyacres Lincoln, who came back to England in 1952. That is one of the reasons that this single and particular bloodline is of such interest to pedigree enthusiasts.

The thirties seem to have been rather a barren era for Mastiffs, although there was one kennel belonging to a Col. Parker, who had considerable numbers of both Mastiffs and Bullmastiffs. The Parkhurst dogs were the sires of the Canadian Mastiffs who were sent to the UK after the war, but not a great deal is known about them.

The next event of major importance was the donation of four Mastiff pups, by Mrs Heather Mellhuish of British Columbia, to England immediately post war. These puppies were, in fact, very inbred as the littermates, Heatherbelle Sterling Silver and

Heatherbelle Portia, were by a Parkhurst dog out of a bitch called Heatherbelle Lady Hyacinth. The other two pups (Heatherbelle Bearehills Rajah and Amelia) were by a dog who was litter brother to Silver and Portia's father, and the dam was a litter sister to Lady Hyacinth. Even so, as has already been said, they were invaluable in saving the breed from extinction. Although the Heatherbelles had Canadian fathers and were born in British Columbia, they go back to American dogs – in fact Heather Mellhuish obtained her foundation stock from Merle Campbell of Oregon.

Betty was lucky enough to meet Heather Mellhuish when she visited British Columbia in 1980, and found her a most interesting and knowledgeable lady. Although she had ceased breeding Mastiff in the mid-sixties, she still had Mastiffs as pets and said she would not be without them. She is still alive and well, and she still has her Mastiffs.

Mastiffs in Canada during the fifties, sixties and seventies were not numerous, and breeders were few and far between. It was not until the formation of the Canadian Mastiff Club that interest was revived. In 1980, while judging the Rottweiler Club of Canada Specialty Show, Betty was approached by people interested in the breed, and in 1985 was invited back to run a seminar for all interested parties.

This proved to be a great success with Mastiff owners coming great distances to attend. In fact, Betty was told that every Mastiff owner in the eastern part of Canada was there. The French Canadian contingent spent fourteen hours on the road non-stop, and a French Canadian dog belonging to Yves Pelletier, Ch. All for a Buck, was the star of the show. The newly formed Mastiff Club was very well satisfied with the results of this happy get together, and with the attendance of nearly twenty Mastiffs, which was a record number.

Although Canada does not have the same density of population as the United States in either humans or Mastiffs, there is a good deal of interest in the breed and Canadian Mastiff breeders often travel considerable distances to show their dogs in America. Two of the most well-known Mastiff kennels in the country at the present time are the Yarrville dogs, belonging to Juanita Voyce, and the Solstice Mastiffs, owned by Kay Langshaw. The Canadian Mastiff Club is forward-looking and enthusiastic, and its president, Bev Malloy, takes an active part in the Mastiff scene as a whole.

Chapter Three

THE MASTIFF IN THE NINETIES

Mastiffs have found their way into many countries over the years, and in world terms the breed is in a state of considerable strength as we go into the last decade of the twentieth century. The future appears be rosier than at any time in the history of this ancient breed, but although numbers are strong, it is essential that the quality of the stock is closely monitored. All breeders have a huge responsibility to preserve the Mastiff to the best of their ability; we should seek to improve the breed where possible, in terms of soundness of conformation and temperament, but we should never seek to change it or undermine it.

NORTH AMERICA

We have looked at the breed in North America historically, and the position seems to go from strength to strength. There have been a few new imports from the UK, and this may help to keep the Mastiff true to type. Understandably in a continent as vast as North America, there are varying opinions as to which stud dogs have made a particular impact on the breed. There are some dogs which are much more generally regarded, and this would include Ch. Gulph Mills Mulcher, who sired almost fifty Champions to many different bitches. Ch. Deer Run Wycliffe was possibly the greatest American sire, and he is behind many of the recent imports into the UK from America. Needless to say, there are many other Mastiffs, too numerous to mention, who have contributed to the breed.

Development of individual type is a matter of selection and dedication. Bob Silvaggi sought out the type he favoured, and then he worked over a long period of time to develop this into a long line of sound, quality dogs. His efforts have had a strong leaning on one UK import, Ch. Gildasan Roman Warrior, a descendant of Canonbury, Rhosnessy and Buckhall lines, who went, unusually, to the United States as a young adult, imported by Pam Gould (Greenbranch). In the UK one of David's dogs is a descendant of Roman Warrior, and puppies from this line have recently been re-imported into America. As has happened in the past, Mastiffs go full circle.

EUROPE

Europe, including Scandinavia, is a huge territory, but although thinly distributed, there are Mastiffs in virtually all the main European countries, especially France, Germany, Holland and Belgium, with smaller numbers in Switzerland, Italy, Spain and Greece. Some Mastiffs have found their way to the former Eastern Bloc countries, but little is heard of progress there so far. The former USSR has recently come into the arena, and in the UK enquiries have been made for first-class stock, but this development is still in the preliminary stages. Scandinavia has a small but dedicated band of enthusiasts, and they have imported Mastiffs from the UK and from mainland Europe, and no doubt they will breed some useful stock as time goes by.

Very few of the European countries have imported stock from the United States. In the main part, the breeders seem to be almost unaware of the great popularity of the breed in the US, and the wealth of bloodlines which is available. However, the cost of travelling to view the stock, coupled with the cost of shipment, can prove prohibitive.

THE PROBLEMS OF IMPORTING STOCK

France, Germany and Holland, especially, have imported Mastiffs from England over the period from the Second World War to the early eighties, but the overall quality was very poor indeed. The lack of a large breeding pool cut down the chance for breeders, however keen or selective, to produce any outstanding specimens. From time to time some winning dogs came up to a reasonable standard, but it was not until some better stock arrived that the standard started to improve by leaps and bounds. There are two fundamental reasons for these sub-standard imports. Firstly, the importers in Europe mostly purchased without visiting England. Potential purchasers would write circular letters to all the Mastiff breeders they could find, or perhaps select the kennel names which happened to be winning at the time. Unfortunately, the cheapest source often proved to be the most attractive. This practice is still well-known to most English breeders, and all those who care about the breed, hate to see poor quality stock going overseas. The second reason for the sub-standard stock in Europe was the result of puppies being imported to countries

Dutch Ch. Artifax Addendum, a successful show Mastiff, based in Holland. He is a son of Lucky Attempt of Farnaby.

Namous Snax (left) and Masnou Fancy Fair exported to Finland in 1991. It is important that all breeders export their best quality stock.

where the breed was very small, and therefore the gene pool was very limited. Some of the best breeders would offer genuine and helpful advice, and would attempt to send abroad the best possible puppies available at the time. Others were not so kind, and they did not send their best stock, or they would send poor puppies because they did not want to admit that they did not have good quality puppies available.

To any potential importer, we would say: try to find out about the person you are proposing to deal with, speak to the Breed Clubs, or preferably, visit a show or so in the country of your choice. This will give you the chance to meet the breeder and to see the type of stock they are showing, so you can choose the bloodlines you wish to have. There is no point in rushing into a purchase; it is better to wait until the right puppy is ready, even if it means having the puppy sent on to you at a later date.

GERMANY AND BELGIUM

Germany and Belgium do not have large numbers of Mastiffs, and the few breeders have to be extremely careful in their planned matings. There are some super dogs, especially in Germany, mostly bred from recent imports, but there is a tendency to lose the true type. Most of the Mastiffs tend to be very sound; they move very well and have bold temperaments. There is an extreme shortage of qualified breed specialist judges, and so all-rounders do most of the judging. The result of this, as happens throughout the dog world, is that the soundest dogs are put up, accepting the risk of loss of type. All-round judges also predominate in America, but their judges are better trained, and there is a much more extensive gene pool for breeders to draw upon, and so there is less risk of losing type.

Another area of judgement which is having a profound effect on some European countries, especially in France and Germany, are temperament tests. As the name suggests, the idea is to make sure that a Mastiff (or any other Working breed of dog) is capable of fulfilling its original purpose. Hence, the Mastiff is regarded as a guard dog, and is expected to be bold. A Mastiff tends to be a reserved animal who would rather walk around trouble. If, for example, you tied a Mastiff to a post and sent the owner in one direction and another person approached the dog with a baton, the true Mastiff would probably stand his ground, but would not attack. If dogs are penalised for being slightly shy, and are praised if they show untypical guarding behaviour, it is only a short step to encouraging vicious dogs to be bred from. While undue shyness is a fault, and a nuisance, it must be kept in proportion.

FRANCE

France has the highest population of dogs (of all breeds) in relationship to human population in Europe, and there are a reasonable number of Mastiffs. The French

Lesdon Lady Betteresse of Namous was highly successful on the European show circuit.

Family group of Ramuncho Mastiffs in France at the National D'elevage. Ch. Ramuncho des Verts Tilleuls (pictured third from left) and his offspring – all from different litters. Uhanna of Namous (second from left) won Most Promising Youngster at the show before returning to England.

Ch. Kosmoss del Mosset del Lleo taking Best of Breed at the Spanish Mulosos Club Championship Show, 1991.

have been fairly prolific importers of the breed from England for some twenty years, but the imports have tended to be a mixture from good and bad breeders. In fact, the French have imported some of their best stock from Holland during the seventies. The Namous and Masnou Mastiffs were resident in France from 1979 to 1983, and when Lesdon Lady Beteresse of Namous was being shown on the European circuit, she was almost unbeatable, with her superb, typical head and massive body.

When she was mated to the French-bred dog, Ch. Ramuncho des Verts Tilleuls, she produced several big winners, who inherited the type and head. One dog who remained in France, Ch. U'King Kong of Namous, was a prolific sire and has been a tremendous influence on the breed. Uhanna of Namous won 'Most Promising Youngster' at the Club Special Show just before returning to England; Ch. Upjoice of Namous was campaigned in the North of Europe; and Ch. Uberacht of Namous had a long and very successful show career in England. The descendants from this mating still strongly influence the stock at Namous/Masnou kennel in England, and the influence is very strong in France and elsewhere. Several Bulliff puppies have also been sent to France, and some interesting crosses between the Bulliff/Namous bloodlines have produced some super Mastiffs, setting the standard for the future.

*Italian Ch.
Damaria Bryn
Fain: Best in Show
winner.*

SPAIN, ITALY AND SWITZERLAND

These countries have very small numbers of Mastiffs, but in the last decade some dedicated dog lovers have taken the breed to their hearts, and several good youngsters are being shown. Again, there is a lack of breed specialist judges, but these Mastiff enthusiasts are to be encouraged in their efforts to introduce and spread the interest in the breed. Much of their stock comes from the Bredwardine, Bulliff, Farnaby and Namous kennels, and their top breeders are to be seen at Crufts as well as some of the Breed Club shows in England, keeping in touch with developments in the breed's home country.

Damaria Powerful Magic,
exported to Australia, pictured at
eleven months.

AUSTRALIA AND NEW ZEALAND

These two countries tend to be looked at together, although they are a fair distance apart, because the two countries tend to pool their resources when it comes to dogs. Along with America, Australia has a long-standing relationship with Mastiffs, unlike most other countries where the explosion in population is quite recent.

The first mention of Mastiffs in Australasia appears in a book by Walter Beilby, entitled *The Dog in Australasia*, published in 1897. In this book there is a very interesting pedigree of a dog called Tirrita Blue Peter, which goes back to the very early English dogs, eg. Thompsons Rose (1800), Lukeys Countess, Crown Prince,

*Aust. Ch.
Damaria
Princess
Zena.*

*Ch. Darkmask
Silver Thorn
pictured at
Alice Springs.*

Turk, etc. Beilby gives details of a dog show held in 1864 where, he says, there were four Mastiffs entered under the name of Lion, three Countesses, two Dukes, and two Barons – which doubtless led to a certain amount of confusion. Beilby also contends that prior to 1882, there were very few good Mastiffs to be met with.

As in the United States, the breed died out in the early part of this century and was not revived until well after the Second World War, with importations from the UK. When Betty was researching Mastiff pedigrees, she came to an absolute dead end with a bitch called Fanifold Undine. Her mother was a Canadian bitch, Heatherbelle Priscilla's Martha, imported immediately post-war by Dr Andy Mayne. Betty was absolutely delighted, and a little surprised, in 1978 to get a letter from a Dr Mayne, now in Australia, enquiring about the possibility of importing a Mastiff bitch. This was the same gentleman, owner of the Fanifold kennels, who had gone to Australia in the early sixties, and was now thinking of starting up in the breed again. It would appear, therefore, that although there was a lapse of some years between emigrating and getting another Mastiff, Dr Mayne has been involved with Mastiffs longer than almost any other person in the world, and certainly longer than anyone else in Australasia.

The first import from the UK was in 1960, but it was in the 1970s and 1980s that numbers of imports increased substantially. There have also been a small number of imports from the United States. A number of kennels have been influential in the breed in Australia over the years, and these would include: Douglas Mummery with the Heatherglens, Amasha Caffn with her Hunzeals, Mr and Mrs Cunson and the Kalcavaliers, and Dr and Mrs Mayne, who kept the Fanifold prefix. In the show ring Ernie Warren has had a great deal of success with some Kalcavalier stock, together with the Belbine and the Calleys.

A very successful Mastiff Club of Australia and New Zealand has been formed and keeps owners and lovers of Mastiffs in contact over the vast distances involved. In late 1992 the name was changed to the Mastiff Club of Australia Inc., reflecting the changing scene in the two countries. The problems of organising entries for dog shows, and social get-togethers are enormous with so much travelling involved, but the club members do surprisingly well, and a quarterly newsletter helps to keep people in touch. In the very recent years, some of the states have set up local Mastiff Clubs, but even in a state such as New South Wales, there may be only thirty members with their Mastiffs, and they may live several hundreds of miles apart.

Although Australia and New Zealand are grouped together, it is important to remember that imports from one to the other are treated as such, and are the subject of great interest when they first appear. In July 1990 the inaugural meeting of The Mastiff Club was held in New Zealand, with fourteen persons present, with the aim of covering New Zealand as a separate entity. To date, there are about fifty Mastiffs in this country.

Kennels in Australasia are generally small, with people usually keeping one or two dogs. Mastiff owners in Australia do face many difficulties with long journeys to get to shows, or to go to a stud dog, and there is a shortage of judges who really know the breed. However, the Mastiff supporters are all keen to learn, and they are determined to get their breed better known.

Chapter Four

CHOOSING A PUPPY

IS A MASTIFF THE BREED FOR YOU?

Mastiff puppies are irresistible: they are cuddly bundles with beautiful, appealing eyes. The first rule must be to resist the temptation to make a hasty decision to buy a puppy without weighing up all the pros and cons. Do not buy a puppy of any sort if your partner is half-hearted about the purchase – it must be wanted by the whole family.

All breeds have their drawbacks, and you should be aware of these before taking on the responsibility of owning an animal. Mastiffs tend to slobber excessively, and when a Mastiff shakes its head, the best advice is to take cover, as slobber may well end up on all four walls and even on the ceiling! You will probably have soggy patches on the arms of your favourite chair, where the Mastiff rests its head – and given half the chance, most Mastiffs prefer an armchair to the floor. You will certainly find out who your real friends are when they first encounter Junior!

With a Mastiff, it is vital that the prospective owner has some idea of how big the dog will grow so that living space and feeding bills can be taken into consideration. In fact, this is a difficult question to answer. The British Breed Standard makes no mention of size or weight; it merely states: "the larger the better". The American Breed Standard stipulates a minimum height for dogs of 30ins at the shoulder, and 27.5ins for bitches. As far as weight is concerned, the guide is "massive and heavy-boned". Generally speaking, a stud dog will weight 200lbs or more, and a good female will reach 180lbs. There is, of course, a terrific variation. Betty had a wonderful brood bitch who weighed no more than 150lbs, and she also had a bitch

Namous Mistress Magdalene. Mastiff puppies are very appealing, but remember just how big they grow.

who weighed in at over 200lbs. Her largest male weighed 220lbs, and at the other end of the scale, she has a very well-made, well proportioned male who was only 150lbs as an adult. It is equally difficult to estimate height. This can range from 28ins at the shoulder to 36ins – or even more.

Never try to get weight on your Mastiff too young, and never let it become overweight. An overweight dog is often an unhealthy dog, and it is better for a Mastiff to be slightly on the lean side. Even if this goes slightly against them in the show ring, they tend to live longer. It is virtually impossible to quote exact quantities that are needed to feed a Mastiff – we are dealing with living creatures, not dummies, and each dog is different. The best advice is to feed to the dog's appetite, and all food, whether you feed fresh meat, canned meat or complete diets, should be of excellent quality. A Mastiff will eat far more when it is young and growing, than it will as an adult. Some get through 6-7lbs of food a day, while others do well on 3-4lbs per day. It is truly a matter of commonsense, and you should be guided by how your dog looks. A Mastiff should not appear thin, but it should not put on so much weight that it is to the detriment of the dog's overall health.

As a general guide, a growing puppy should receive four meals a day, with each meal weighing about 1lb. If the puppy still appears hungry and is not putting on weight, the quantity should be increased. Adults should be fed two meals a day, one smaller than the other. The small meal usually weights about 1 1/2lbs, and the larger meal around 2 1/2lbs.

PET OR SHOW?

Most newcomers to the breed start off by saying that they want their Mastiff as a pet, but quite often they start to get interested in the breed. They join a breed club, attend a few shows, and before they know it, they have caught the show-going bug! Obviously the cost of purchasing a show prospect may be higher than the cost of a pet, but you should always try to get as good a puppy as you can afford – good in both type and temperament. If you buy a show quality Mastiff puppy, you do not *have* to show it, but if you buy a Mastiff as a pet and later decide that you want to show it, you may find your dog is not up to the required standard. If this should happen, do not feel badly; beauty is in the eye of the beholder and your Mastiff must not be loved any the less if unsuccessful in the show ring.

MALE OR FEMALE?

Whether you choose a male or a female Mastiff is entirely a matter of personal preference. Without doubt, the male is larger, more imposing and stronger than the female. The bitch tends to be gentler in nature; she is not quite so big and she may be more affectionate – though the desire to give and receive love is a strong Mastiff trait, whatever the sex. Bitches are often quieter and more responsive than dogs, but you do have the problem of the bitch coming into season. With a large breed such as the Mastiff, bitches do not come into season as frequently as they do in smaller breeds; every ten months would be the norm for a Mastiff. If there are no plans for breeding, the owner then has to ensure that the bitch is isolated from males for a two-to-three week period. As far as children are concerned, both male and female Mastiffs are equally tolerant.

CHOOSING A BREEDER

One of the best things you can do to is get in touch with a breed club, and find out when and where they are holding a show. Be prepared to travel a fair distance, both

When you are choosing a puppy, it helps if you can also see the parents to assess looks and temperament. This family group shows (left to right) Lesdon Lady Betteresse of Namous and young puppies, Uhanna of Namous and U'King Kong of Namous – puppies from an earlier litter – and the father, Ch. Ramuncho des Verts Tilleuls.

to visit a show and when it comes to visiting breeders, because Mastiffs do not grow on trees. Club Shows tend to be fairly informal, subject to Kennel Club rules, and you can watch the judging, and talk to the exhibitors, and you have a chance to view the various bloodlines being shown. Talk to the exhibitors who enjoy their showing and do not necessarily breed themselves: they will give you hints and tips on which bloodlines are the most reliable, without prejudice.

You may well find that various dogs you like may appear to be unrelated, but, if you look at the pedigrees, you will find many common ancestors. It is a good idea to obtain a copy of the Breed Standard, and to go through it carefully, so that you can decide in your own mind which dogs come nearest, in your opinion, to the Standard. This will give you a guide as to which kennel to approach with a view to obtaining your puppy.

When you have decided which colour you prefer, whether you want a male or a female, and which particular type of bloodlines you want, keep in touch with the breeders you feel you can best rely on, and be prepared to wait for some time until your choice can be fulfilled. Many kennels are run on a small scale, and may well only have one or two litters per year. Be patient – after all, you will hopefully have years of companionship from your Mastiff, so it is worth waiting that little while extra to get what you want.

Do beware of pre-judging the exact features you wish to have in your puppy, because each and every puppy is a little character all its own, and you may overlook the best puppy which is nearest to your ideal, just because it happens to fail in one minor detail. This is especially important in an eight-week-old baby, because Mastiffs change dramatically from week to week as they grow, and they do go through some absolutely dreadful stages. The experienced and helpful breeder will guide you and give an honest opinion of how the puppy is likely to be when it is adult. When you go to inspect the litter, you should be able to see the puppies' mother, and perhaps the sire will also be there. Take note of the breed type and the temperament of the parents, and try not to choose a puppy whose mother is very nervous. Calm, friendly parents produce calm, friendly puppies.

How do you know if the breeder you have chosen is helpful and honest? This is where you can be helped by the secretary of the breed club: a breeder who cares enough about the general welfare of the breed is almost certain to be a full member of the specialist breed clubs, because by this means they will learn about new findings in animal health, and potential problems in particular bloodlines. The club secretary will know the members who are really responsible, and, while a particular person cannot be recommended, you will be pointed in the direction of those people who take their breeding seriously.

In every country there are people who decide to breed purely for the profit. In some cases, this may mean that they skimp on rearing costs and leave the mother to feed and care for the puppies for too long, and this means the pups will end up as weaklings, and will never fulfil their potential. For the truly dedicated breeder, money always come second to the desire to produce healthy, bonny puppies – and it always shows.

BREED POINTS

What you are looking for, primarily, is a healthy puppy that is of good size for its age, with dense bone, and a nice disposition. When you see the puppies for the first time, look at them with a detached eye, watch quietly how they react with each other and with things about them. Mastiff puppies are naturally inquisitive, but they are not always that bold, especially with newly-encountered people. Most Mastiffs are quite quick to approach 'things', but are often very slow with people.

If you put a cardboard carton in the middle of the lawn, more often than not a Mastiff puppy will quickly go up to it and will possibly climb inside it. However, if a stranger is sitting next to the box, it may take ten minutes of circling, sniffing, and thinking, before the approach is made. This is quite natural in the breed.

A beautiful Mastiff head. This puppy, pictured at four months, is Uhanna of Namous who went on to win Most Promising Youngster awared at the French Mastiff Club Special Show.

The puppy should have a good square and heavy head; even at a young age the head is the most impressive characteristic, and a good Mastiff puppy leaves you in no doubt as to what breed it is. The body should be quite heavy and tends to be rather short in the young, lengthening out as the dog develops in later months to the correct proportions, as laid down in the Breed Standard.

Beware of a really heavy coat; while some Mastiff babies have a soft, slightly silky puppy coat, long-coats do turn up from time to time. These range from slightly heavy-coated to absolute balls of fluff. Some judges will penalise a heavy coat, whereas others will look at the animal as a whole and feel that the coat is minor compared with more fundamental issues. Real 'fluffies' cannot be shown, and should not be bred from, as this is a genetic fault which is best avoided. Having said that, if you are looking for a family pet, and you have no intention of breeding or showing, a fluffy will make a superb companion, and should come much less expensive than a show specimen.

If you read the Breed Standard several times – and you really should – you will be

Watch the puppies at play, and you will get some idea of temperament.

able to see the essence of the breed characteristics in the puppy and to talk to the breeder about each feature, as some bloodlines do develop at a completely different rate to others. Do not be downhearted if your puppy looks completely immature when compared with others the same age in the ring. Often the dog which matures quickly, and looks adult by ten or fifteen months will be an old has-been by the time it is three years old, whereas the slow-maturing dog will look its best at four years, and will still be a winner at nine.

Ask the breeder whether the puppy has been wormed, and when, and also find out whether it has had any inoculations. Depending on the age that you collect the puppy – and normally this is at about eight weeks of age – primary inoculations should have been given to cover the puppy for the first week or so in its new home; the final ones are given in a couple of weeks time. When the time comes for you to go and collect the latest member of your family, you should be given a diet sheet, a pedigree, and, if possible, the registration form. This may, however, come a little later, as sometimes the Kennel Club takes a few weeks to issue these forms. Of course, you will have checked and double-checked that the parents themselves are KC registered.

You should also ask the breeder whether the parents have been X-rayed for hip dysplasia. This is a condition that can affect large, heavy breeds, and although it is not as prevalent in Mastiffs as was thought at one time, some breeders, though not all, X-ray to see that their breeding stock is 'clear'. In the UK most good breeders insure their puppies for the first six weeks of their new lives, and this gives security all-round.

Finally, remember you are getting what you hope will be a loyal, loving, healthy, happy and protective companion, for whom you will be responsible for the next ten or twelve years; so it is worthwhile taking a good deal of trouble to be sure of getting the right animal. Never be tempted to take one that is not 100 per cent fit and well. A great deal of attention to detail before buying can save so much heartache later on.

Chapter Five

TRAINING AND SOCIALISATION

The first thing to say on the subject of training and socialisation of young puppies, is that it is largely a matter of common sense. You have a young creature, dependent upon your care and affection, and you must start the way you intend to go on. Kindness, gentleness, coupled with firmness, are the key notes. The first thing to do is introduce your new baby to the bed area. Let your pup know that this space, whether in the kitchen, annexe, or wherever, is where it has to sleep. Make sure your Mastiff has a warm soft bed, in a quiet spot. And from an early age do make sure that when told to go to bed and stay there, your pup does so!

HOUSE TRAINING

Much has been written on the subject of house training and, again, this is truly a matter of common sense. Mastiffs are generally clean, and if a puppy is put out immediately upon waking, and after each meal, and praised when performing outside, it will soon get the idea. If the pup is shut up in a kitchen at night, put newspaper down, and this will help to limit the area that is soiled. A puppy will not be able to remain clean all night long before the age of four months. The secret is to catch the puppy when it is just about to have an 'accident' indoors, and then go outside with a bit of a scold in your voice. When the puppy has done what you want outside, reward with plenty of praise, and then take the pup back in the house again.

LEAD TRAINING

Lead training again often causes some upsets. The first step is to put a very light collar on your puppy and leave it on for a while, ignoring shakes and scratches. A

Kindness, gentleness, coupled with firmness are the key notes when training a Mastiff puppy.

soft leather collar is best; never leave a choke chain on a puppy, or adult dog for that matter, if you are not with your Mastiff. Serious accidents can happen with a collar that can tighten if it gets caught in something.

When the collar has been accepted, attach a length of cord, and let the puppy walk around, trailing it on the ground, for a little while each day. Then you can start to pick up the cord and call the puppy to you, praising when it comes, and perhaps giving a small reward.

Your puppy may well act like a bucking bronco when first walked with on a lead. Just stand still, talk gently and encouragingly, and wait until the pup calms down. Again, most Mastiffs accept a lead quite happily, only too pleased to be going out

Lord Hunky Chunky of Masnou, a son of Galbren Golden Gancy of Masnou, pictured at nine weeks.
Start off by using a soft, leather collar on your Mastiff puppy.

with their owner. Whether you choose a soft, leather lead or a nylon lead is a matter of personal preference. We tend to favour a leather lead (3-4ft in length), with a good, strong clip. Beware leads with metal links in them as these can take the skin off your fingers if the Mastiff gives a sudden plunge.

CAR JOURNEYS

It is a good idea to get your puppy used to travelling in the car from an early age. Nearly all Mastiffs love cars; they know it means that they are going somewhere for a nice walk. Car sickness does not seem to be a problem with the breed.

Mastiffs should always travel in the rear of the car, installed behind a strong dog barrier. This is not only to stop the dog from climbing on the back seats; it is an essential safety measure. If the car has to stop abruptly it could throw the Mastiff on top of the driver, which could be extremely dangerous for all concerned. If you travel to shows with more than one dog, it is advisable to install wire crates in the rear of the estate car or van. These can be made to measure, or bought ready for installation, but do make sure they are properly fixed in the vehicle.

THE IMPORTANCE OF SOCIALISATION

There are two things to remember with a young Mastiff, which appear diametrically opposed. First, you must not over-exercise your puppy while it is still young. The bone is very soft, and the dog must not be put on a lead and made to walk from point

Mastiffs crave human companionship, and usually love children.

A rope-tug is an ideal toy for a Mastiff puppy.

A to point B. The pup can play at will in the garden, but should not be stressed by being taken for walks which may be far too long.

However, the opposite side of the coin is that it is absolutely essential that a Mastiff puppy is socialised. This is a breed that is highly likely to become nervous and neurotic if it is just left at home and not allowed to meet people. With today's anti-dog climate, it is also more difficult to get strangers to stroke or fuss over a puppy.

Betty takes her puppies up to the village and sits on a seat in the square, and just lets the puppy watch people come and go, and, with luck, people come up and make a fuss. The railway station, or the the local pub, are also useful places to visit – anything to enable the puppy to meet people and see the outside world. The best home for a young Mastiff is one with children, of sensible age, who have friends in and out of the house, so that there is always hustle and bustle about the place, and the dog doesn't have an opportunity to sit alone and be isolated from the outside world.

If you have a local dog training class, it is a good idea to go along, once the inoculations programme has been completed. It is not necessary to join in, but if you sit with your puppy and watch everything that is going on, the pup will meet people who like dogs, and will also see lots of other breeds.

Mastiffs are a wonderful breed, but they do crave human companionship. They are not the slightest use to themselves or anyone else if they are shut away and not allowed to make friends; so make sure that your Mastiff is truly a member of your family. Nervousness in Mastiffs can be hereditary, but a good deal is due to environment.

Play is an important part of development, and all puppies like toys – and so do many adult dogs. However, care must be taken that the toys cannot disintegrate. The best type seem to be the big, heavy rope 'tugs' which seem to defy all manner of treatment! Hide chews, so beloved by smaller breeds, can be dangerous for a Mastiff. If the chew is torn apart by a strong-jawed Mastiff it becomes a long, supple piece of hide, and if this is swallowed, the dog could easily choke.

Beware of balls that can be taken completely into the dog's mouth. If a Mastiff manages to catch a ball of this size, it could easily get stuck in the back of the dog's throat – and the results would certainly be fatal. With a breed that is so big and powerful, the owner needs to take special care in order to prevent accidents occurring. The majority of toys which are perfectly safe for smaller breeds, are not suitable for Mastiffs. The best toys to provide are big balls, and big rope tugs – anything that is large and tough.

TRAINING

Remember that when your Mastiff is fully grown there is no way that you will be able to force the dog to obey, so you must start treating the dog right from the beginning as you mean to go on. If your puppy is too rough and too bossy, don't just laugh it off as puppyishness. Perhaps it is, but always remember what that sort of behaviour would be like when the dog is an adult. A firm "No" has to mean No. Don't be like a mother in the supermarket with a complaining child continually asking for sweets; she says "No" ten times and then gives in for the sake of peace and quiet. If you do this with a puppy, you are asking for trouble.

If you say "No", and mean it, then that has got to be it. If the pup is really naughty, hold the dog by the sides of its cheeks and give it a good shake and scold in a loud voice. This is what the pack leader in any dog or wolf pack would do, and the young dog accepts it. There is no need to be unkind, but you must be firm. Usually a harsh voice is all that is needed, as Mastiffs are extremely sensitive, despite their size, but just occasionally a little more discipline is required.

In America, the use of a crate is more commonplace than it is in Britain, and it forms a standard part of the 'home' equipment. Puppies are often trained to stay in their crates for set periods of the day. This gives puppies a place to rest – and they are also kept out of mischief for a time! This way puppies have a room of their own.

Mastiffs are generally wonderful with children. The only trouble is their propensity for 'giving the paw', which can scratch the face of a small child. As for guarding, they are excellent because of their size and depth of bark. They are not normally fierce, and their usual trick is to let somebody into the house but then, if they are on their own with no human to give an order, they will not let the 'visitor' out again. Betty recalls coming home to find that two friends from Canada had let themselves in unannounced. They had gone into the front room and her dog, Sheba, had plonked herself down in front of them. They were 'doggy' people, but every time they moved she just gave a little growl and glared at them. They had sat there all afternoon by the time Betty got home from work!

Most Mastiffs are very tolerant of smaller dogs, or any other pets, as long as the Mastiff is brought up with them. It would not be advisable to introduce an adult Mastiff into a home where there are cats or rabbits, or any other small pets. A Mastiff can be trained to live peaceably alongside such pets, but to be entirely trustworthy, the Mastiff should have been brought up with the pets that are to share the home.

The same applies if another adult Mastiff is introduced to a home; this can be a cause of some jealousy, whereas in ninety-nine cases out of a hundred an adult Mastiff will accept a puppy, of either sex. As a breed, Mastiffs are generally tolerant creatures, although some bitches find it hard to look lovingly on Toy breeds – or they look on them too lovingly as far as the Toy dogs are concerned! Males tend to be more phlegmatic, and are more likely to accept smaller dogs. Betty's huge stud dog, Ch. Parcwood W. Bear Esq of Lesdon, has been seen plodding along with a Jack Russell Terrier hanging from his neck, utterly ignoring his attacker – almost as if he couldn't be bother to make any response.

As with all dogs, Mastiffs must learn to fit in with their owners and their owners' wishes. They must learn to come when called, to lie quietly at home, and to be left for short periods of time. They must learn not to bark and not to run off, or do anything else that the owner deems as unacceptable. A Mastiff, being so big and heavy, has to learn all this while still small enough to be instructed gently but firmly. Most Mastiffs are patient and gentle, and devoted to their owners, but they can also be stubborn. In most instances, this is because the Mastiff has failed to understand what is required. Generally, Mastiffs have an intense desire to please, and they crave human affection and companionship. If you sit down, your Mastiff will come and lean against your legs – your dog wants to be with you, to be stroked and loved, and should never be disappointed.

It is important to bear in mind, that a big, heavy Mastiff cannot move as quickly as a small dog. Mastiffs need time to turn, to sit, and get their act together. That is why the breed is unsuitable for Obedience competitions. Mastiffs are perfectly capable of performing the exercises, but it has to be at their own time and at their own pace. Obedience judges are so used to seeing the lightning reactions of Border Collies and other Obedience-orientated breeds, that a big, slow dog is likely to be penalised for not being so quick or so precise. The Mastiff owner should therefore aim for basic obedience. A well-trained Mastiff should respond to such commands as "Sit", "Stay", "Come", and the dog should fit in with the owner's life, but do not expect your Mastiff to react quickly. A loving, dignified, lifelong friend is what you have with a Mastiff, and it is up to you, the owner, never to let your dog down.

Chapter Six

CARING FOR YOUR MASTIFF

Mastiffs generally lead a very healthy life, free from any major problems. However, all dogs need to be fed, exercised and cared for correctly, and with a big dog such as a Mastiff, there are certain factors to bear in mind. Throughout your Mastiff's life, you should take a note of any changes in general appearance and behaviour, as this can be the first signs of some impending problem. If you are worried, a quick word with your vet may either put your mind at rest, or mean that a medical problem is spotted early and is therefore easier to treat. Coat condition can be a useful guide to general health. If your dog is fed a good diet, and is in good condition, the coat will be smooth to the touch, and look healthy. A staring, harsh-feeling coat could mean a dietary or a medical problem. The diet could be lacking in oil content, and a little vegetable oil added to his food (approx 10ml per day) should quickly restore the coat to full condition.

There are a number of areas where all dogs needs regular care and attention, which we will deal with one at a time.

FEEDING
Diet for the adult Mastiff has changed over the decades, but never so much as in the last ten years. Traditional foods were raw meat plus plain wholemeal biscuit (or baked-up bread rusk) with a varied assortment of vitamin and mineral additives. This was all very hit and miss, and it really was a matter of luck whether your dog had a balanced diet or not. It is amazing how fit and well developed some of those old-time dogs were, against all the odds.

This situation has now changed drastically. Complete diets are readily available in all major countries, and they really are complete. The daily requirements are scientifically established and blended in the feeds in the correct proportions, in a manner which is easily and properly assimilated by any breed of dog. However, we would dispute claims that since a big heavy dog eats more than a tiny one, the diet needed is exactly the same, and only differs in quantity. In fact, a Mastiff, despite its eventual size and weight, eats less than some very energetic dogs of less bulk.

When complete diets were first introduced, many of the established breeders were very sceptical, but now most people use complete feeds with total satisfaction. In fact, not all complete feeds are new. At least one English company has been making a complete, dry diet for over a hundred years!

Since each feed has its own qualities, it is impossible to specify brands, besides which, many are available in certain countries only. But we can only stress that you should choose a brand which suits your dog's individual needs. It is no use buying the best, most expensive brand, if your dog will only eat it under protest. It is better to buy a slightly lower quality diet which your dog enjoys, and therefore eats in sufficient bulk to keep healthy. As with puppies, you should aim for fitness without fatness. No one wishes to see Mastiffs which are lean and hungry, showing all their ribs and haunches, but nor do we wish to see rolling fat. The Breed Standard calls for substance, but this is not the same as fat. Substance is a composite of flesh and muscle on a well-formed and well-matured frame.

No matter what you feed your dog, fresh water must be available at all times, and Mastiffs probably drink more than many other similar sized breeds. If you find the dog is drinking to excess and has a tummy that looks like a water bag, ask your vet to check for any problems such as liver or kidney complaints. It is also worth looking at the type of food you are using, in case it is causing metabolic imbalance. Many breeders prefer a type of food you can soak before use, which ensures that it is fully swollen before entering the stomach, and you are therefore sure that your dog is not subject to dehydration. Some breeders feel that feeding dry foods without soaking can add to the risk of bloat, due to the extra fermentation and gas activity in the stomach, and some feed manufacturers do accept this could be a possibility.

If you feed a complete feed, strictly spreaking, you should add nothing, as this will cause some imbalance in the nutritional composition of the diet. However, it is quite acceptable to use a little gravy, or a little meat of some sort, simply to add flavour to what otherwise could become a boring regime. Just imagine if you ate your favourite dish for every meal, every day of the year – you would become fed up with it in no time!

It is best to mount the feed bowl at a raised height from the floor, since a large dog reaching down to eat from the floor places the food tract at a strange angle, and

Mastiffs do not require a lot of exercise when they are young.

indigestion or ingestion of air can occur which is not ideal. A height of about twelve inches (30cms.) from the floor is fine for a mature Mastiff, and placed a little lower for youngsters. A raised dish means that puppies (or the family cat) cannot get involved, so the risks of fighting over food are reduced.

EXERCISE
Mastiffs do not need very much exercise when they are young. A puppy will play for a while, then have a little rest, or even go to sleep, and then start to play again. In the garden, your dog will stroll about quite happily, but will often stop and sit or lie down, in the most peculiar of places, for a little rest, or a think! When you take a puppy for a walk, you will find that it will be happy to walk with you, and will continue for a considerable distance, but you will then notice that it is becoming increasingly tired – and by then it is too late; the puppy will have exhausted its reserves of strength, and may be damaging its soft bones and developing muscles. There is a good chance that you are still far from home, so even more damage could result.

The answer is that you do not take a young mastiff "out for a little walk". Training sessions should be confined to short sessions, in and around the home. Alternatively,

A Mastiff's favourite exercise is to sit down and watch you work!

you can take your puppy in the car to a suitable spot where a little play and training can take place, then allow time for a rest. Never, ever, let your young Mastiff become exhausted. You will find, as time goes by, that little excursions do not tire the puppy, and by about six months you can start *short* walks, especially as part of the socialisation development, and this can be gradually increased as the puppy strengthens up. However, it is worth remembering that a Mastiff's favourite form of exercise is to sit down and watch you work! If you are working in the garden, your puppy will follow you around, and will then find a favourite spot to sit or lie down, and will be content to watch you for long periods. When you move, the pup may eventually get up and plod around for a while, and will then settle nearer to you for a while. Equally, your Mastiff may wander off to explore some other item of interest, and demonstrate that Mastiff speciality – temporary deafness!

Most enthusiasts will tell how a Mastiff can totally ignore you, despite all calls, offers of rewards or whatever, even if the dog is normally the most obedient animal. This is not disobedience – but a Mastiff will get totally engrossed in some little matter of great importance, and seem to shut out all else. In these situations, if you ignore the dog, it will suddenly come to you with a hurt look, as though you were the guilty party!

COAT CARE

Mastiffs do not need constant grooming or bathing. A quick daily brush or comb through will keep loose hair from being left around the house, on the furniture. Do not brush or comb too harshly, as the skin is quite sensitive and it should not be scratched or damaged. Some Mastiffs do shed more hair than others. The fawns appear to have a slightly heavier undercoat, which does come away like a fluff, whereas the brindles have less undercoat, but sometimes a slightly heavier, coarser, main coat, which may shed less. Mastiffs moult each spring and autumn, and while this is much less than many other breeds, you will need to give your dog a little extra attention at these times in order to to reduce the problems of dog-hairs on carpets and furniture.

BATHING

A Mastiff should not be bathed too frequently, as this would have an adverse effect on the natural oils in the coat. An annual bath should be sufficient. It is better to bath outdoors, when the weather is warm. The best method is to have a bucket of warm water, and the water should be gently ladled over over the dog's back and worked into the coat, prior to applying the shampoo. There are various types of shampoo available, depending on the state of the dog's coat. Insecticidal shampoos incorporate agents to kill fleas, ticks and other skin parasites, and if properly applied, they can be very effective as part of a general hygiene routine. Other shampoos can help with dry skin, sensitivity and allergy problems, and certain of the excemas. Always follow the directions carefully, as some of these products are very concentrated and can cause more problems than they solve, if incorrectly used.

Work the shampoo well into the undercoat, making sure the coat is thoroughly wet. Lather right through to the skin, especially if you are using shampoo to deal with a problem, and work up a good lather. Do take care not to get any shampoo in the dog's eyes, nor in the ears. Once you have worked the shampoo into the coat, leave it for a few minutes, and then add a little more water and work up a further lather before rinsing off with ample warm water. Some products, and some people, recommend repeating the shampoo treatment, using less shampoo the second time, to ensure thorough cleansing. Whether you do this, or you decide that one shampoo is enough, it is essential to ensure that you rinse every bit of shampoo out of the coat by using plenty of water.

Your Mastiff should then be rough-dried with a towel. If the weather is mild, you can leave the dog to run about in the fresh air, and it will soon get dry. However, if the weather is inclement you will need to dry the dog with a towel, and then use a hair-dryer. This can be a specialist dog-dryer, or a conventional hair-dryer, but it is important to make sure that the dog does not get too hot. When your Mastiff is dry, a careful combing and brushing will remove all the loose fur, leaving your dog sweet-smelling and feeling nice and fresh. If you have a shower in your home, which is easily accessible, this can be more convenient than using buckets of water. However, beware of taking your Mastiff upstairs, as a wet dog returning downstairs can get water everywhere!

TEETH

In general, a Mastiff has little tooth trouble. Hard biscuits to chew on will keep unhealthy deposits away. Choose a biscuit which is large enough so that a Mastiff cannot easily swallow it whole. We find that a chewy type of rubber or nylon bone-shaped toy will also encourage hearty chewing for hours on end. Do be prepared, though, for slobber. All this chewing and working on a non-destructible toy will make those saliva glands work overtime, so perhaps this is a pleasurable pastime for the garden. It may become necessary to have the teeth cleaned by the vet, but this should *not* become a regular habit just to keep the teeth looking spruce. You can try a toothbrush and toothpaste if you wish. There are specially designed canine toothbrushes and toothpastes available. Again, this can be a messy business. In old age the teeth will get less exercise. They may become a little soiled, which can lead to bad breath. If there is some problem, such as tooth decay, the dog may need to have teeth removed, but this should be a last resort. We have found that most Mastiffs enjoy fruit, and if a dog is given an apple to chew it can help to keep teeth clean and breath sweet-smelling.

EARS

Ears must be kept clean and healthy, and Mastiffs have few problems in this area. However, if the environment is excessively dusty, or your dog runs regularly in vegetation and grass, there is a good chance that dirt and seeds will find their way into the outer ear, causing irritation and possible infection if left unattended.

The best way to clean ears is to use a small piece of cotton wool (cotton) or a cotton bud and carefully wipe out the outer folds of the ear to remove dust and dirt, and any excess wax. If you find that there is an offensive smell, or if there is a dry, bloody deposit around the folds, the dog may have ear mites. These are minute spiders which live in the deepest reaches of the ear, and will cause problems if they are not eradicated. The vet will supply a treatment of drops, and these must be dripped into the depths of the ear. These will kill the intruders, and clean the inner areas of the ear. Continue to clean the outer areas, but *never probe into the ear*, as great damage can be done, even by cotton buds.

Mastiffs like somewhere soft to lie, but it is a matter of personal preference whether you allow your dog on the furniture.

NAILS

If Mastiffs are exercised regularly on a hard surface such as concrete, their nails will naturally keep fairly short. However, if they lead a 'soft' life, going from carpet to grass, their nails may need a little trimming from time to time. It is worth getting the puppy used to this at an early age.

The ideal tool for the job is a strong pair of nail-pliers, as supplied for human toenails. An electrician's wire-cutter or a tool of similar design will also do the job. There are also a number of different types of canine nail-clippers available. The aim is trim off the light-coloured, almost transparent point, taking great care not to cut or damage the blood-carrying 'quick'. If in doubt, ask your breeder or your vet to show you how to perform this simple operation.

BEDDING

Your Mastiff will love somewhere soft and warm to lie down. It is a matter of personal preference whether you allow your dog to sleep in an old armchair, or whether you supply a box or a specially manufactured dog bed, but it is essential that the bed is situated somewhere that is draught-free. There is no need to buy anything special or expensive; a Mastiff will soon feel at home, once your dog knows where to sleep.

There is a variety of bedding to choose from. Again, an old blanket draped over the armchair or in the dog bed, is sufficient, as long as it is washed regularly. A wooden box or platform can be scrubbed out with a disinfectant, but do be careful to rinse any chemicals away before returning it to use. In the box you can use a blanket, a piece of soft (not nylon) carpet, or one of the modern fleece materials. All these different materials can be laundered easily, and so you can keep the bed fresh, and free from odours. Beware of bean bags containing huge quantities of polystyrene beads; they can take months to clear up if the bag is punctured, either by accident or if it is chewed!

KENNELLING

Mastiffs are best in the home with their family, but if you do need to keep them outside, please do not shut your dog outside for long periods. If you intend to keep Mastiffs as kennel dogs you will miss much of the unique character and the great loyalty they show to their people. Any outside kennel must be dry and draught-free, and provided with suitable bedding at all times. You can use shredded paper as a bedding material, but make sure that it is soft paper (most computer paper is unsuitable). The disadvantage of shredded paper is that the dog may decide to carry it about in mouthfuls. This can result in a terrible mess, which is difficult to clear up, especially when the paper is soiled or wet.

WORMING

When you buy your Mastiff, the breeder should tell you when the dog was last wormed, and the treatment that was used. There are several 'all-in-one' wormers available today, and these seem to have a wide variation in their effect, depending on the species of worms present.

ROUNDWORMS: This is the most common type of worm in dogs, and can sometimes be seen when immature or dead worms are passed with the motions. A dog infested with roundworms may lose condition, or it may eat well but fail to maintain reasonable weight. Alternatively, some dogs with worms have a poor appetite and refuse food regularly. If your dog takes to sitting on its bottom and dragging its rear along the ground, this is a sure sign of irritation of the anus by worms of one sort or another. Luckily, roundworms are easy to treat, in tablet, paste or syrup form, and your vet can recommend the most suitable product.

TAPEWORMS: These come in several species, and some are very difficult to clear. Signs of infestation are normally when segments released by the worm are passed in the dog's motions. These are like small grains of rice, and can often be seen to be moving slightly. However, some varieties are almost microscopic. Tapeworms cannot be 'caught' by one dog from another – they are passed on by other hosts, such as fleas; so obviously eradicating flea infestation will minimise the risk of tapeworm infestation.

There are tablets manufactured specifically to treat tapeworms, or you can use a multi-wormer, although these are not as effective in their action. There are also injections which can be administered by the vet, and these are reported to be very effective, but they are costly. Some varieties of tapeworm can be almost impossible to clear, and in extreme cases, where there is no effective treatment, a dog may have to be put down, but luckily, such worms are not too prevalent.

HOOKWORMS AND THREADWORMS: These are quite rare in most countries, but they do turn up in some areas, and if they are suspected, the vet should be able to supply a suitable wormer.

In all cases where worms are suspected and treatment does not appear effective, a stool sample can be analysed by a veterinary laboratory, so that the exact species can be determined, and a specific treatment can then be prescribed.

Chapter Seven

THE BREED STANDARD

THE DEVELOPMENT OF THE MASTIFF

Anybody interested in the breed is bound to ask: How have we got the Mastiff that we see today? What has gone into the making of our dogs? Have they reached the final stage of their development, or will we try to alter them to suit our own requirements?

Although Mastiffs were originally Dogs of War and Baiting Dogs, they have always been primarily guards of people and property. The description by Conrad Heresbatch, published in 1586 in the *Foure Bookes of Husbandrei*, is still relevant today: "His disposition must be neither too gentle nor too curst, neither fawn upon a thief or fly for his friends". These dogs were almost certainly not as huge as today's Mastiffs; they were probably lighter and quicker, and certainly fiercer, but similar in many respects. Throughout the ages, dogs were kept and bred for what they could do, and not necessarily for what they looked like – that change occurred with the formation of the Kennel Club and the start of exhibiting dogs in shows.

We have made our Mastiffs bigger, heavier, stronger, perhaps less mobile, and certainly milder in temperament. How closely the type resuscitated by enthusiasts in the early 1800s resembled their forebears in all points, it would be hard to say. Our present Mastiffs in some ways resemble those that were being produced at the beginning of the 19th century, although they are unlike in other ways. For example, with the introduction of St Bernard or Alpine blood, bone became denser and heads broader and wider, and muzzles deeper. All changes have come about gradually over the years and not, of course, overnight. Attitudes have also changed towards dog-keeping, and today's Mastiff is the result of years of careful breeding.

Ch. Farnaby Fraze and Fable: Mastiff Bitch of the Year 1990. A typical example of the Mastiff today, bred for size, docility and massiveness.

Pearce.

We have a breed, which, despite the outcrosses which have proved necessary upon occasions, is a very ancient and very honourable one. We have bred for size, docility, and massiveness, while still trying to retain the admirable characteristics which have made the Mastiff, throughout the ages, a superb guard and companion. The finished product certainly resembles pictures of Mastiffs of one hundred years ago – and even those of two hundred years ago, in most respects, while differing in others. We must always remember that we have an enormous responsibility towards this wonderful breed, and hopefully, where changes have taken place, they have been for the better.

It must be said that after the Second World War, the dire shortage of breeding stock and the resulting massive in-breeding meant that soundness in the breed was very bad. If a dog had a pleasing head and looked good while standing, then it would win, even with appalling movement. Today this attitude is, thankfully, a thing of the past, and movement is generally sound. After all, it is no use having a wonderful-looking dog who is a cripple, but conversely it is no use having a dog that can move like a dream who looks like a Great Dane and has no breed type.

It is certainly difficult to get everything that is is required: breed type, soundness and good temperament, but these are the criteria that today's breeders must bear in mind. Despite the changes which we have made, we *have* kept the original type of dog, and we can look back through many hundreds of years of history and realise that our Mastiff of today does go back to the 'dogs of the Ancient Britons'. And what we have now, we should try to keep. We do not need more changes, and we now have enough breeding stock to make outcrosses unnecessary. Today's Mastiff is the amalgam of all that has gone before, and as such is something to be greatly valued.

DRAWING UP THE BREED STANDARD

It is obvious that a Breed Standard is no less than the actual blueprint of the breed. The English Mastiff Breed Standard was drawn up in the very early days of the Old English Mastiff Club, in the last century, and has remained virtually unaltered ever since. This particular Standard is one of the very few that makes no mention of height or weight. Most Standards in other countries, especially those that are members of the FCI, are based on the English Standard (as the breed's country of origin), which is then translated into the native tongue. The ideal type in Europe is, therefore, exactly what you would expect to see in any English Championship Show. However, there are very few breed specialist judges available, so most of the judging is by all-rounders, who again tend to 'spot' the showy, good-moving dog, and often dogs of superior type are passed over in favour of lighter, less typical specimens.

The Europeans also have what are, in effect, 'notes for judges' which lay down certain details which are considered criteria essential to the breed. One of these refers to 'Bite', where judges are told to penalise an undershot jaw, and, as is usual with the Europeans, all teeth should be present in the jaw, to the extent that if teeth are missing the animal can be barred from breeding, and cannot become a Champion.

Some countries, such as France, have a system of 'Confirmation' in order for dogs to be passed fit for breeding. A dog or bitch must either be placed 'Very Good' or higher, or be examined by a breed expert in order to qualify. The persons authorised to carry out confirmations are registered by the French Kennel Club (SCC) and are either breed specialists who have to undergo a course of training, or the All-Rounders licensed for the particular breed. While this does have some pitfalls, at least most of the Mastiffs used for breeding are of reasonable quality.

Australia and New Zealand have very few Mastiffs. Both countries currently use the English Standard without change, although some changes are being discussed. The American Breed Standard follows the British Standard closely, with a few notable exceptions.

THE BRITISH BREED STANDARD

GENERAL APPEARANCE
Head, in general outline, giving a square appearance when viewed from any point. Breadth greatly desired; in ratio to length of whole head and face as 2/3. Body massive, broad, deep, long, powerfully built, on legs wide apart and squarely set. Muscles sharply defined. Size a great desideratum, if combined with quality. Height and substance important if both points are proportionately combined.

CHARACTERISTICS
Large, massive, powerful, symmetrical, well-knit frame. A combination of grandeur and courage.

TEMPERAMENT
Calm, affectionate to owners, but capable of guarding.

HEAD AND SKULL
Skull broad between ears, forehead flat, but wrinkled when attention is excited. Brows (superciliary ridges) slightly raised. Muscles of temples and cheeks (temporal and masseter) well developed. Arch across skull of a rounded, flattened curve, with depression up centre of forehead from median line between eyes to halfway up sagittal suture. Face or muzzle short, broad under eyes, and keeping nearly parallel in width to end of nose; Truncated i.e. blunt and cut off squarely, thus forming a right-angle with upper line of face, a great depth from point of nose to underjaw. Underjaw broad to end. Nose broad with widely spreading nostrils when viewed from front, flat (not pointed or turned up) in profile. Lips diverging at obtuse angles with septum, and slightly pendulous so as to show a square profile. Length of muzzle to whole head and face as 1/3. Circumference of muzzle (measured mid-way between eyes and nose) to that of head (measured before the ears) as 3/5.

EYES
Small, wide apart, divided by at least space of two eyes. Stop between eyes well marked but not too abrupt. Colour hazel brown, darker the better, showing no haw.

EARS
Small, thin to touch, wide apart, set on at highest points of sides of skull, so as to continue outline across summit, and lying flat and close to cheeks when in repose.

MOUTH
Canine teeth healthy; powerful and wide apart; incisors level, or lower projecting beyond upper but never so much as to become visible when mouth is closed.

NECK
Slightly arched, moderately long, very muscular, and measuring in circumference about one or two inches less than skull before ears.

FOREQUARTERS
Shoulder and arm slightly sloping, heavy and muscular. Legs straight and strong and set wide apart; bones being large. Elbows square. Pasterns upright.

BODY
Chest wide, deep and well let down between forelegs. Ribs arched and well rounded. False ribs deep and well set back to hips. Girth one-third more than height at shoulder. Back and loins wide and muscular; flat and very wide in bitch, slightly arched in dog. Great depth of flanks.

HINDQUARTERS
Broad, wide and muscular, with well-developed second thighs, hocks bent, wide apart, and quite squarely set when standing or walking.

FEET
Large and round. Toes well arched. Nails black.

TAIL
Set on high, and reaching to hocks, or a little below them, wide at its root and

tapering to end, hanging straight in repose, but forming a curve with end pointing upwards, but not over back, when dog is excited.

GAIT/MOVEMENT
Powerful, easy extension.

COAT
Short and close-lying, but not too fine over shoulders, neck and back.

COLOUR
Apricot-fawn, silver-fawn, fawn, or dark fawn-brindle. In any case, muzzle, ears and nose should be black with black round orbits, and extending upwards between them.

FAULTS
Any departure from the foregoing points should be considered a fault and the seriousness with which the fault should be regarded should be in exact proportion to its degree.

NOTE: Male animals should have two apparently normal testicles fully descended into the scrotum.

Reproduced by kind permission of the English Kennel Club.

THE AMERICAN BREED STANDARD

Effective from December 31 1991.

GENERAL APPEARANCE
The Mastiff is a large, massive, symmetrical dog with a well-knit frame. The impression is one of grandeur and dignity. Dogs are more massive throughout. Bitches should not be faulted for being somewhat smaller in all dimensions while maintaining a proportionally powerful structure. A good evaluation considers positive qualities of type and soundness with equal weight.

SIZE, PROPORTION, SUBSTANCE
Size – Dogs, minimum, 30 inches at the shoulder. Bitches, minimum 27.5 inches at the shoulder.

Fault – dogs or bitches below standard. The further below standard, the greater the fault.

Proportion – Rectangular, the length of the dog from forechest to rump is somewhat longer than the height at the withers. The height of the dog should come from depth of body rather than from length of leg.

Substance – Massive, heavy-boned, with a powerful muscle structure. Great depth and breadth desirable.

Fault – Lack of substance or slab-sided.

HEAD

In general outline giving a massive appearance when viewed from any angle. Breadth greatly desired.

Eyes – Set wide apart, medium in size, never too prominent.

Expression – Alert but kindly. Colour of eyes brown, the darker the better, and showing no haw. Light eyes or predatory expression is undesirable.

Ears – Small in proportion to the skull, V-shaped, rounded at the tips. Leather moderately thin, set widely apart at the highest points on the sides of the skull continuing the outline across the summit. They should lie close to the cheeks when in repose. Ears dark in color, the blacker the better, conforming to the colour of the muzzle.

Skull – Broad and somewhat flattened between the ears, forehead slightly curved, showing marked wrinkles which are particularly distinctive when at attention. Brows (superciliary ridges) moderately raised. Muscles of the temples well developed, those of the cheeks extremely powerful. Arch across the skull a flattened curve with a furrow up the center of the forehead. This extends from between the eyes to halfway up the skull. The stop between the eyes well marked but not too abrupt. Muzzle should be half the length of the skull, thus dividing the head into three parts, one for the foreface and two for the skull. In other words, the distance from the tip of the nose to the stop is equal to one-half the distance between the stop and the occiput. Circumference of the muzzle (measured midway between the eyes and nose) to that of the head (measured before the ears) is as 3 is to 5.

Muzzle – Short, broad under the eyes and running nearly equal in width to the end of the nose. Truncated, i.e. blunt and cut off square, thus forming a right angle with the upper line of the face. Of great depth from the point of the nose to the underjaw. Underjaw broad to the end and slightly rounded. Muzzle dark in color, the blacker the better.

Fault – Snipiness of the muzzle.

Nose – Broad and always dark in colour, the blacker the better, with spread flat nostrils (not pointed or turned up) in profile.

Lips – Diverging at obtuse angles with the septum and sufficiently pendulous so as to show a modified square profile.

Canine Teeth – Healthy and wide apart. Jaws powerful. Scissors bite preferred, but a moderately undershot jaw should not be faulted providing the teeth are not visible when the mouth is closed.

NECK, TOPLINE, BODY

Neck – Powerful, very muscular, slightly arched and of medium length. The neck gradually increases in circumference as it approaches the shoulder. Neck moderately 'dry' (not showing an excess of loose skin).

Topline – In profile the topline should be straight, level, firm, and not swaybacked, roached, or dropping off sharply behind the high point of the rump.

Chest – Wide, deep, rounded and well let down between the forelegs, extending at least to the elbow. Forechest should be deep and well defined, with the breast bone extending in front of the foremost part of the shoulders. Ribs well rounded. False ribs deep and well set back.

Underline – There should be a reasonable, but not exaggerated, tuck up.

Back – Muscular, powerful, and straight. When viewed from the rear, there should be a slight rounding over the rump.

Loins – Wide and muscular.

Tail – Set on moderately high and reaching to the hocks or a little below. Wide at the root, tapering to the end, hanging straight in repose, forming a slight curve, but never over the back when the dog is in motion.

FOREQUARTERS

Shoulders – Moderately sloping, powerful and muscular, with no tendency towards looseness. Degree of front angulation to match correct rear angulation. Legs straight, strong and set well apart, heavy boned.

Elbows – Parallel to body.

Pasterns – Strong and bent only slightly.

Feet – Large, round, and compact with well arched toes. Black nails preferred.

HINDQUARTERS

Hindquarters – Broad, wide and muscular.

Second Thighs – Well developed, leading to a strong hock joint.

Stifle joint – Is moderately angulated matching the front.

Rear Legs – Are wide apart and parallel when viewed from the rear.

When the portion of the leg below the hock is correctly 'set back' and stands perpendicular to the ground, a plumb line dropped from the rearmost point in the hindquarters will pass in front of the foot. This rules out straight hocks, and since stifle angulation varies with hock angulation, it also rules out insufficiently angulated stifles. Fault – Straight stifles.

COAT

Outer coat straight, coarse and of moderately short length. Undercoat dense, short, and close lying. Coat should not be so long as to produce 'fringe' on the belly, tail, or hind legs.

Fault – Long or wavy coat.

COLOR

Fawn, Apricot, or Brindle. Brindle should have fawn or apricot as a background color which should be completely covered with very dark stripes. Muzzle, ears, and nose must be dark in color, the blacker the better, with similar color tone around the eye orbits and extending upward between them. A small patch of white on the chest is permitted.

Faults - Excessive white on the chest or white on any other part of the body. Mask, ears, or nose lacking dark pigment.

GAIT

The gait denotes power and strength. The rear legs should have drive, while the forelegs should track smoothly with good reach. In motion, the legs move straight forward; as the dog's speed increases from a walk to a trot, the feet move in toward the center line of the body to maintain balance.

TEMPERAMENT

A combination of grandeur and good nature, courage and docility. Dignity, rather than gaiety, is the Mastiff's correct demeanor. Judges should not condone shyness or viciousness. Conversely, judges should also beware of putting a premium on showiness.

Reproduced by kind permission of the American Kennel Club.

Anatomy of the Mastiff

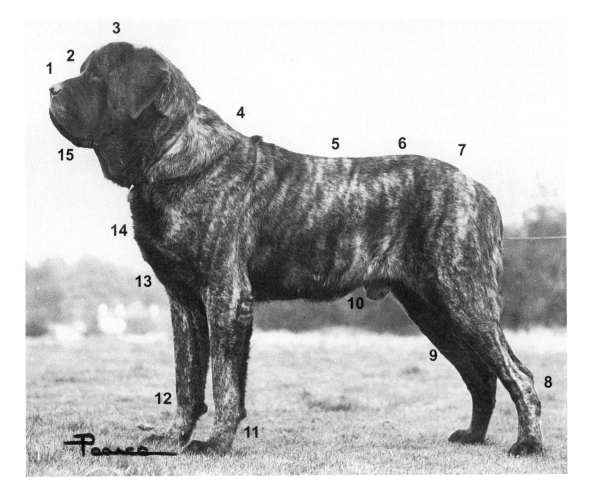

Key to anatomy

1. Muzzle
2. Stop
3. Occiput
4. Withers
5. Back
6. Loin
7. Croup
8. Hock joint
9. Stifle
10. Tuck up
11. Front pastern
12. Pastern joint
13. Chest
14. Shoulder
15. Flews

INTERPRETATION OF THE STANDARD

GENERAL APPEARANCE

The British Breed Standard does not give specific guidelines to size and weight; it simply requests a "large, massive, powerful, symmetrical, well-knit frame." We are therefore looking for a very large, very powerful, and very massive dog, but the massiveness and height must come from the depth of the body rather than the legs, in the approximate proportion of two-thirds body to one-third legs. A Mastiff should not be too tall and gangly. The American Breed Standard asks for dogs to have a minimum height of 30 inches at the shoulder, and bitches should be 27.5 inches.

TEMPERAMENT

The Mastiff has a very loyal temperament; this is simply described in the British Standard as "Calm, affectionate to owners, but capable of guarding." There is a little more detail in the American Standard, and words such as 'dignity' and 'courage' build up a good picture.

Several countries are introducing 'Temperament Tests' as part of the qualification towards gaining the title of Champion, and this is normally included in the Club Championship Show. This can lead to problems if a dog is rewarded for showing aggression, as can be the case. While it may be right to penalise a dog which is a quivering heap in the ring, no matter how good it may otherwise be, we do not want to go to the opposite extreme and encourage a dog to attack as proof of its 'guarding' abilities. The American Standard specifically states that "Judges should not condone shyness or viciousness."

HEAD

The Mastiff is an extremely 'head conscious' breed, and the description of the head forms the largest part of both the British and the American Standard. It is, however, quite difficult to visualise if one is not familiar with the breed.

It is the head which really makes the Mastiff; it must be big, broad and flat across the skull, with the ears set on at the highest point so that the line across the ears and skull is continuous. The stop between the eyes must be pronounced, not shallow, and the muzzle itself must be very broad and very deep – these two proportions should be almost the same. So many Mastiffs have muzzles which narrow and appear to taper, or which are not filled out under the eyes, giving a weak appearance. It should, as the British Standard says, be blunt, cut off squarely. The length of the muzzle to the whole head should be as 1 to 3.

One very important point here is the question of wrinkle, and this differs between

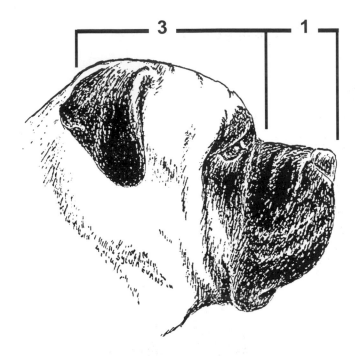

Correct head proportions, seen in profile.

Correct head proportions from the front.

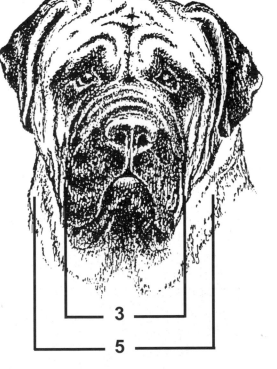

Mastiffs heads, all showing excellent type

Farnaby Merrick.

Farnaby Front Runner.

French Ch. U'King Kong of Namous.

The British Breed requires the Mastiff's head to be dry, with the wrinkle making all the difference to the dog's expression when it is attracted, as shown by Erohito de Belgodene at Masnou, aged twelve months.

The American Breed Standard calls for "marked wrinkles which are particularly distinctive when at attention", as shown by Mistletoe Let It Ride.

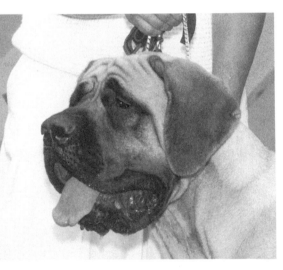

the British and the American Standards. The British Standard asks for the forehead to be flat but wrinkled when alert, whereas the American Standard calls for "marked wrinkles which are particularly distinctive when at attention". This one small phrase does make quite a difference to the appearance of heads. As far as the British Standard is concerned, this should mean that the head should be comparatively 'dry', with the wrinkle making all the difference to the dog's appearance and expression when the ears are raised and the dog is interested or excited. In British show rings this is being wrongly interpreted, and too many Mastiffs are showing a continually wrinkled head, combined with excessive folds of flesh down the sides of the cheek, making the Mastiff look rather like a Bloodhound. The difference

Head faults

Long snipey muzzle.

Domed skull, low-set ears.

Muzzle too short.

Round prominent eyes, showing haw.

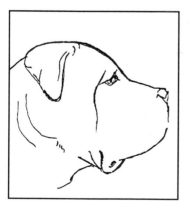

Plain head, lacking stop.

Narrow muzzle, lacking underjaw.

Head faults

Long houndy ears.

Excessively undershot.

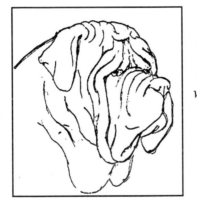

Over-wrinkled.

between the correct amount of wrinkle and too much wrinkle can make all the difference to the overall picture.

To summarise, the two main faults that are seen in the show ring are narrow, weak muzzles and over-wrinkling. Of the two, the snipey, weak muzzle, lacking strength under the eyes, should be more severely penalised. However, the appearance of the head, in its finer points, has been interpreted in many different ways by many different people. All one can say in conclusion is that breeders, judges and exhibitors must be governed by the requirements of their national Breed Standard, which stipulates the correct and desired type of head. The Breed Standard is the blueprint, and it should be followed in all its details.

EYES

Eyes should be small, set wide apart and dark in colour. There must not be red haw showing. The ears should be small and thin to the touch; again heavy ears are a common fault.

MOUTH

Again, we have a variation between the British and American Standards. The American Standard states that a "scissors bite is preferred" although a moderately undershot jaw should not be faulted. The British Standard states that the lower jaw may project beyond the upper, "but never so much as to show when the mouth is closed." This means that the Mastiff is, quite legally, allowed to be slightly undershot, but so many judges and even breeders do not appear to realise this. However, it should be obvious that the very short, blunt, broad muzzle – which is absolutely essential – is very difficult to combine with a scissor bite.

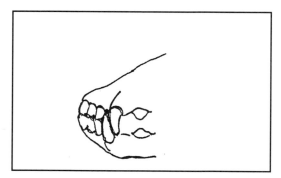

Level bite: desirable.

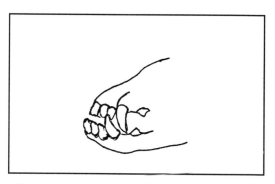

Slightly undershot: allowable.

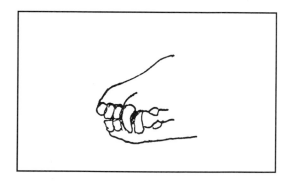

Overshot: incorrect.

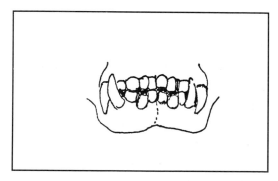

Teeth out of alignment.

A fawn Mastiff showing correct proportions and outline. Note the broad, deep chest.

BODY

The body slightly longer than high, not square like a Bullmastiff. This is a very common fault, and some judges even praise the cobbiness of their winners, but this is certainly not a desirable attribute.

The chest must be broad and deep – as the saying goes, "you don't want two front legs coming out of the same hole." When viewed from the front, the chest must indeed be very broad and should come down at least level with the elbows. This will not be apparent in young dogs, but when a Mastiff is fully mature the chest must be well let down between the front legs so as to be level with the elbows. The topline must be flat, and very wide in a bitch. It should be slightly arched in the dog.

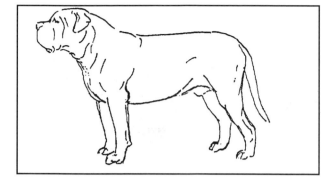

Correct: long body, level topline.

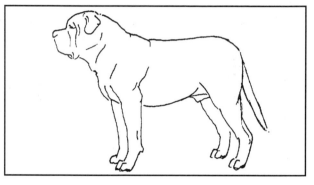

Short body giving square appearance. Tail set too low.

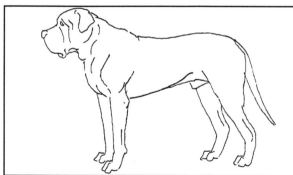

Lack of depth; too Dane-like.

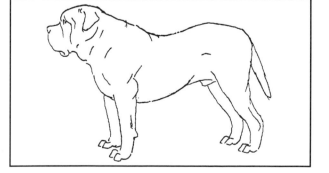

Dipping topline, tail too short.

This brindle Mastiff shows a body that is slightly longer than high, which is correct for a Mastiff. It must not appear square, which is typical of the Bullmastiff.

FOREQUARTERS

The shoulders should be well-laid; they should not be upright – this is a bad fault. Upright shoulders may make for greater height, but the front action will suffer. Remember that the pasterns – the shock absorbers – will find it more difficult to absorb jarring from movement with upright shoulders, as the jolting leads straight down the shoulders into the front legs. In the Breed Standard the pasterns are required to be "upright", but even so, there should be a degree of flexibility. Correct pasterns and correctly placed shoulders give the essential cushioning to the heavy body when on the move.

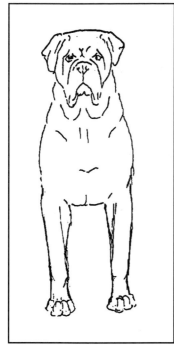

Correct front.

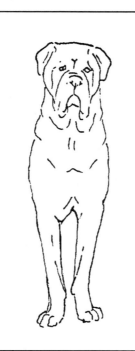

*Narrow front,
feet turned out.*

*Out at elbow,
feet turned in.*

*Correct
upper arm
and
shoulder.*

*Straight
upper arm
and
shoulder,
short neck.*

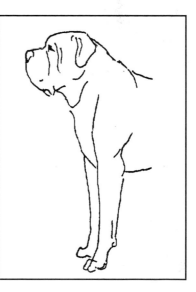

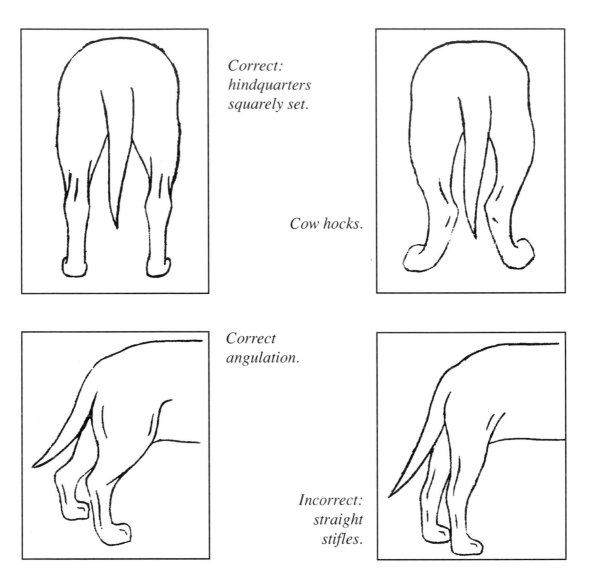

Correct: hindquarters squarely set.

Cow hocks.

Correct angulation.

Incorrect: straight stifles.

HINDQUARTERS

The hindquarters must be strong, with a good bend of stifle. The American Standard asks for the stifle joint to be moderately angulated, matching the front. The British Standard does not mention this angulation at all. It calls for hindquarters to be broad, wide and muscular, and the second thigh must be well developed. It seems obvious from this that angulation should be good, and not straight up-and-down like a Chow Chow. However, these straight and narrow hind legs are a common fault in the breed. Viewed from the side, the back end should resemble that of a shirehorse rather than a racehorse.

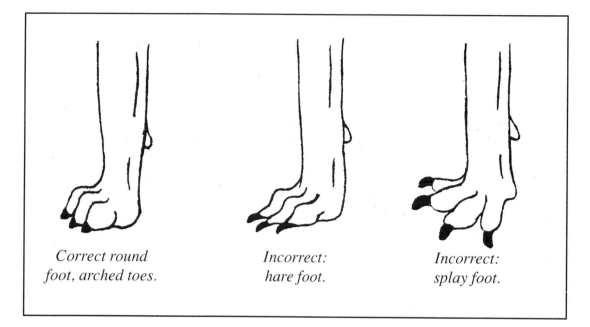

Correct round foot, arched toes.　　*Incorrect: hare foot.*　　*Incorrect: splay foot.*

FEET

The feet should be round and cat-like; they should not be spread out or hare-like. These feet bear a tremendous amount of weight and must be up the work entailed. The nails should be dark in colour and kept short. In show stock the dew claws are often removed when the puppy is a day or two old, but if these are not removed they must be watched to make sure they do not grow and curl round, sometimes back into the leg.

TAIL

The tail is set on high, and should be carried straight, but with a little curve upwards on the move or when excited. A low-set tail means that the hindquarters seem to slope away downwards, instead of being level and straight into the tail-set. The croup or rump must be strong and straight, and should not fall or slope away. Some years ago it was common to find a 'cranked' tail in one or two puppies in a litter – a throwback to the Bulldog – but these are now very rarely seen.

COAT AND COLOUR

The coat should be short and close lying, but is allowed to be heavier and thicker over the shoulders, neck and back. There is a great deal of variation in coat lengths, from the really long-coated (due to the St Bernard ancestry, probably) to the Doberman type of coat. However, the 'moderately short' coat is correct. Although

A long-coated Mastiff – a legacy of cross-breeding with St Bernards. The correct length is "moderately short".

officially there are only three colours in the breed – fawn, brindle and apricot – there can be quite an amount of variation in the fawn and brindle colours. The fawn can vary from very light, which used to be called silver-fawn, to much darker bordering almost on the red of the apricot, or a donkey-brown. Brindles also vary from being very nearly black in colour all over, with just a very few faint stripes, to an apricot brindle where the stripes are a very attractive apricot colour. However, a 'reverse brindle', where you have a light background (instead of a dark background) with a very few faint stripes of another colour is not desirable.

GAIT
The British Standard confines itself to "Powerful, easy extension", whereas the American description of movement is far more detailed. A Mastiff should move powerfully and freely, but it should not be expected to move like a racehorse, or a

Great Dane. It should move not with grace, but with strength. The movement of a Mastiff can be likened to the earth-shattering movement of a Shire Horse. You cannot expect a dog of this build to move in any other way.

SUMMARY

It has to be admitted that other breeds have, of necessity, been used in saving the Mastiff, and so often these breeds have characteristics which are diametrically opposed to those required in the Mastiff. The St Bernard has a long coat and very often carries white markings; the Bullmastiff is square and has an ultra short muzzle; the Newfoundland has a shallow stop; the Bloodhound has far too much wrinkle; the Dogue de Bordeaux has liver pigment and yellow eyes. You only need just one dog of any breed to introduce something which is alien to the Mastiff, and future breeders have a very difficult job to breed it out over succeeding generations.

Chapter Eight

THE SHOW RING

Unless a Mastiff puppy is bought specifically to be shown, the chances are that any such idea will be initiated by a friend saying: "That's a lovely dog, why don't you show it?" This sows the seed of interest and the wish for further information. The owner becomes intrigued, and wants to find out what is involved in showing a dog: What is a show like? How is it run? What prizes can be won?

A dog show is a beauty show. It can cost a lot of money to enter and the distances travelled can be enormous; but above all it must be remembered that dog showing is a sport. It is not the be all and end all, it is not a matter of life and death. If you can go to a dog show, fail to be placed in the ring but still enjoy the day, then you have the right sort of outlook and temperament.

THE BRITISH SHOW SYSTEM

Dog shows are run by canine societies, of which there are hundreds, under the rules and regulations of the national Kennel Club, the canine world's ruling body. In Britain there are Exemption Shows, Open Shows and Championship Shows, and it is at the latter, larger and more important events that Champions are 'made up'. To become a Champion, a dog must be the best of its sex in its breed at three Championship shows and under three different judges. Entries can run into scores, if not hundreds, so it is far from easy to make up a Champion.

Dog shows are divided into various classes: puppy, which is for dogs from 6-12 months; junior, for dogs up to 18 months; and thereafter classes are graded by the number of first prizes an animal may have won, up to the Open class, which as its name implies is open to all. If you are contemplating entering your dog at a show, then it would be advisable to go to one or two shows without the dog, just to see for yourself what happens, before deciding whether or not this sport is for you. Details of shows are given in the dog papers or in your breed society newsletter. Breed societies hold shows just for that one breed, and these shows are normally relaxed and cheerful affairs, and these are the best sort to attend when you are learning.

In most instances, the judge and steward will enter the ring and the steward will call in the first class and line up the dogs for the judge to inspect. The judge usually walks around, looking at all the exhibits to begin with, and then asks the handlers to move the dogs round the ring. The judge will then call out each dog individually to examine it, and the handler will be asked to move the dog again. After looking at each exhibit, the judge will then place the first four or five in order of merit. The prize cards will be handed out by the steward, and the next class will be called into the ring. The winner of each class, as long as it has not been beaten in a subsequent class, will return to the ring later when the judge decides on the Best of Sex and then Best of Breed. And that, briefly, is how a dog show is run!

THE AMERICAN SHOW SYSTEM

In some ways American shows differ quite considerably from the British equivalent, both in numbers of entries and in the way they are organised. In the USA there are two types of shows: Matches, which are fun events, and Championship shows, which may be Specialty shows (for one breed) or an all-breeds show. The classification usually consists of Puppy, Novice, Twelve to Eighteen Months, Bred by Exhibitor, American-bred and Open, and there is a special class for Champions. The points that are awarded go to the best animal that is not already a Champion, whereas in the UK a dog must beat *all* comers to win a Challenge Certificate. To become a Champion in America a dog must obtain fifteen points, and of these at least two wins must be 'majors' (i.e.of three points each or better) where the dog has beaten a specific number of others in its sex and breed. The beaten dogs do not need to be in the same class as the points winner, they just have to be present and competing at the show.

The value of the points on offer depends on the numbers of that particular breed being shown in any given area. This means that in an area where a particular breed is popular and entries at shows are therefore higher, there must be more animals present at a specific show in order to qualify for a major. So in Colorado, for instance, you might need an entry of only four or five Mastiffs for a three point major to be allocated, whereas the entry on the East Coast might run into higher figures before a three point major is allocated.

American shows are superbly organised, with an AKC representative in

American shows are superbly well organised, as Betty (left) found when she was invited to judge at the Bucks County Kennel Club in 1985. She is pictured with Best of Winners, Deer Run Police.

attendance, ensuring that timetables are adhered to and that the whole show is run efficiently and according to AKC regulations.

SHOW TRAINING

If, after attending a few shows as an onlooker, you still feel that you would like to participate, it should be obvious that you must have a dog which will behave in the ring and not leap around like a mad thing or try to hide when the judge comes to examine. It is a good idea to take all Mastiff puppies to a general training class, in order that they get used to people, other dogs, and a strange environment. They will, hopefully, also learn the fundamental Obedience commands.

However, if you want to show your dog, the next step is to attend a ring training class – most of the bigger general training clubs have a special ring training section. At these classes, your dog will be handled by the trainer and examined all over, including inspection of its teeth. You will also learn how to move your dog, at the correct pace, on a loose lead. If your dog is steady and well behaved, you could go straight from your home into the show ring without any further preparation, but it would be far better, and much fairer to the dog, to have had a bit of practice first.

SHOW PREPARATION

As a smooth-coated breed, the Mastiff is comparatively easy to prepare for the show ring. You can, if you wish, bathe your Mastiff the day before a show, but this is not normally necessary. In cold weather a 'dry' shampoo is probably more advisable than soap and water. In fine weather, it is easiest to bathe your Mastiff outside, using buckets of warm water and a mild disinfectant 'wash'. If you are using soap or shampoo, make sure that it is thoroughly rinsed from the coat, as it could cause irritation.

All dogs should be groomed regularly, and with a Mastiff this should consist of firm (not rough) brushing with a medium hard brush. This should be done before your dog goes into the ring. A last minute polish with a soft, silk cloth or with a chamois leather is all that is needed to make a Mastiff's coat gleam. A little Vaseline, applied to the nose and the toenails, will add the finishing touches. Make sure that the eyes are clean and not at all 'weepy'.

Two other points to bear in mind: toenails should never be allowed to get too long, and anal glands sometimes need to be emptied. The latter is normally a job for the vet.

IN THE SHOW RING

When you enter the show ring with your dog for the first time, you will probably forget all that you have learned, and so it is a good idea to attend a few informal shows before competing at the top level.

When you are showing a dog, it is essential to wear suitable clothing – high heels and jewellery are definitely not required. You will need to run round the ring with your dog, so flat shoes and comfortable clothes are advisable. However, you should try to look smart, and perhaps try to complement the colour of your dog's coat. The aim is to complement the dog, and not to detract from its appearance by billowing skirts or other unsuitable garments.

In America professional handlers are used on a regular basis, largely due to the expense and the distances involved in campaigning a dog. However, in some of the breeds, owners handle their own dogs in the ring. Professional handlers are very proficient, and they make the business of showing more competitive than it is in the UK. The presentation of both dog and handler is immaculate, and British exhibitors could learn a lot from their ring technique.

When you enter the ring, remember to keep your dog on your left hand side, on a

Ch. Mistletoe Flashy Emma: the art of showing a Mastiff is for the dog to stand four-square, showing an interested and alert expression.

WINNERS

TRAP FALLS
KENNEL CLUB
MARCH
1989
JOHN ASHBEY

fairly loose lead. The left side is nearest the judge, of course, as he or she stands in the centre of the ring, and the dogs are placed around the perimeter. After moving round the ring altogether, the dogs are called out one at a time. When your turn comes, get your dog to stand four square, looking alert – and this is easier said than done. Do not let your show prospect keep all four feet close together, looking as if it is standing on a sixpence; let the dog stand with the front legs upright and the hind legs slightly placed back. The whole picture should be of a well balanced dog, not a hunched up fidgeting one.

A Mastiff using ears and looking alert will appear a hundred times better than one with ears back and looking bored. Try to have something in your hand to tempt the dog – a piece of well-cooked liver, or a squeaky toy, perhaps – something to stimulate the dog to look its best when the judge is assessing. After the initial inspection, the judge will then examine the dog: feel the bone, look at the mouth, the eyes, and the hindquarters and testicles (in the case of a male). Thereafter, the judge will probably stand back and just look once more. The dog then has to be moved at a trot, so the judge can assess gait.

After each dog has been seen, the chances are that the judge will stand in the middle of the ring, and ask for all the dogs to be lined up for a final assessment. This is another important moment and, again, the dog should be looking alert and happy. It is so easy to relax too soon – for you and the dog to 'sag', or for the dog to fidget and move from its show stance. You can guarantee that this will happen just as the judge looks in your direction, so make sure that you watch the judge at all times, and that when the judge looks at you and your dog, you are both looking your best.

Always remember that, first and foremost, this is a day out for you and for your dog – something to be enjoyed, not endured. A dog that is nervous and frightened can be coaxed into acceptable ring behaviour, but unless the dog can take the stress and strain, which can be quite considerable, it is far better to leave it at home. If the dog hates showing, it will not really make for a pleasant day for either of you.

Having said this, it must be admitted that most Mastiffs are not naturally extrovert showgoers, like some breeds, and a lot of them have the 'I suppose I must' look about them, and do their best to emulate a sack of potatoes on a lead! If you have a good specimen of the breed, and you have trained your dog to look happy and at home in the ring, then you will both go far. If you really become immersed in the breed, then the show ring will be of great interest to you.

However, showing is certainly not the pinnacle of dog owning. If either of us had to choose between exhibiting our dogs, or just keeping our dogs as pets, then we would both opt for keeping our dogs purely as companions – although we both thoroughly enjoy show-going. Do remember that for the hard core of dog exhibitors,

Galbren Golden Fancy of Masnou at nine months, learning to stand steady for the show ring. Note higher rear end, which is typical of this stage of development.

Alan Walker.

the expenses are high and the distances to be travelled are great. So do not get involved in showing, unless both you and your dog really enjoy it. Once you are bitten by the show bug, it can easily become a way of life, but always make sure that the dog, or dogs always come first.

JUDGING

There is a growing tendency for people to think that they are ready to start judging after they have owned a dog for two or three years, and have enjoyed some success in the show ring. This should not be the case. It takes many years before someone has sufficient depth of knowledge to go into the centre of the ring and assess a class of dogs. This should never be undertaken prematurely, and judging should certainly not be undertaken merely as self-gratification. It carries important obligations, and the prestige of the job should always be of secondary importance to the desire to judge.

In America there are very few breed specialist judges; it is rare for people who are active in the breed as breeders and exhibitors to become judges. American judges are normally multi-breed or Group judges.

All judging, at whatever level, should be undertaken honestly, gently, and calmly, and to the best of your abilities. Judges can do a great deal of harm if they abuse their power, or are not suitably qualified to make a correct assessment. It should always be remembered that judges are ordinary, everyday mortals, dog breeders and exhibitors themselves, who for that one day have a great deal of responsibility thrust upon them. The next week they may well be showing their own dogs under another judge, and be on the receiving end.

So, if you want to show your dog, then do all the groundwork, and ensure that the dog is trained and enjoys the day out as much as you do. Do not get obsessed about winning or losing; take your dog to a show because you enjoy it, and for no other reason – and the best of luck to you both!

Chapter Nine

BREEDING

If you own a pedigree dog, you may well be tempted to breed. After all, you reckon your Mastiff is the best in the whole world, and it seems like a good idea to produce more. This may well sound ideal, but there is more to it than you may think, and it is essential to weigh up all the pros and cons before you become involved in bringing more puppies into the world.

Breeding carries with it tremendous responsibilities, both to the owner of the bitch and the owner of the stud dog, and there are some quite considerable risks to your Mastiff and to your pocket. Responsibilities start from the moment you decide to mate your bitch or use your dog at stud, and these fall into several main categories.

RESPONSIBILITY TO THE BREED
If you breed a litter, you must aim to make an improvement, or at least consolidate the best features of the breed, as stated in the Breed Standard. The dog and bitch that you plan to use must both be assessed with this in mind. Even the greatest experts sometimes make a mistake, and a litter ends up far from what was hoped for, and the breeder has to decide whether to put down most, or all of the puppies, or decide whether they can be safely sold as pets. Are you ready to make these decisions?

RESPONSIBILITY TO THE BUYERS OF THE PUPPIES
You have made decisions which will affect the lives of the puppies, and their new owners. If something does go wrong, are you willing and able to resume responsibility and either take an unwanted dog back, or rehome it?

RESPONSIBILITY TO FUTURE GENERATIONS

Remember, your puppies may be bred from in their turn, and any faults which you have introduced or multiplied will make their presence known for generations to come.

RESPONSIBILITY FOR THE FINANCIAL RISKS

This might occur if, for instance, the bitch needs a major operation such as a caesarian and then produces no live puppies. Vets' fees are not cheap, and you must have the resources to cover all eventualities. If you sell all the puppies and within a short while some, or even all of them die, or have to be put down because of some problem you have perhaps unwittingly introduced, are you able to refund the money and pay any resulting expenses?

Assuming that you have considered all these factors and you are still committed to breeding, where do you go to obtain expert advice in order to avoid as many as possible of the pitfalls? If you have kept in touch with the breeders of your Mastiff, they should know a little of what is involved, assuming that they are responsible and have a planned breeding programme. Attending shows and club seminars will teach you a lot about the Breed Standard – which bloodlines you feel best represent your ideal type, and which particular dogs match particular bitches. Most senior breeders will be happy to discuss aspects of the genetics of your bitch, and will give advice concerning the best alliance for her.

BREEDING PROGRAMMES

The various qualities and defects in the bitch must be considered without any kennel blindness, so that the stud dog you choose hopefully exhibits none of the faults which your bitch has. The perfect Mastiff does not exist, so it is important to assess breeding stock objectively, and try not to to double up on any fault, if you can help it. However, it is important to assess each animal as a whole as well as looking at specific features; you may have to ignore some minor points in order to avoid any major faults in the bloodlines. As part of your decision-making process, you have to consider which breeding programme you want to follow.

LINE BREEDING

Line breeding means that you carefully mate your bitch with a dog from the same bloodlines, such as grandfather to granddaughter. This can be very effective, cementing the good points in a line, *providing* there are no major faults in the background. Breeders undertaking line breeding need to research pedigrees very thoroughly before planning a mating. Initially, it is probably wise to use dogs from the same basic related bloodlines, but keeping to perhaps a common grandparent line. Line breeding is most important in fixing type, and producing a litter where there is a great similarity among the various puppies in the litter.

IN BREEDING
This follows the same principles as line breeding, except that the dog and bitch are even more closely related, such as brother to sister or father to daughter. The chances of doubling up on faults and weakening the line are very high, and it takes a breeder of considerable experience to achieve successful results.

OUTCROSSING
As the name implies, this is where the stud dog and the brood bitch are as far removed in their pedigrees as possible, and you may find that on a three generation pedigree there are no dogs appearing on both halves of the pedigree. This is a safe form of breeding, providing that the two sets of bloodlines are compatible, with as few faults known in any of the dogs on the pedigree. Experienced breeders will know which dogs, or which bloodlines are most dangerous for particular faults and particular virtues, and can make a reasoned judgement as to the likely result on the litter. However, a newcomer to breeding will need to rely on assistance, although even the most experienced person cannot offer a cast iron guarantee. Outcrossing will produce the most mixed litters, where no two puppies may even look alike, but it does offer a wider choice to those wishing to establish a sound basis for their breeding programme. However, it is essential that the puppies are carefully selected, and only the very best kept for future breeding.

BREEDING FOR COLOUR
When you are planning a litter, your first consideration it to find the best match for your bitch in terms of breed points and bloodlines. Breeding for colour is a secondary consideration, but it is worth working out the likely results. However, although these calculations may appear very simple at first, genetics and Mastiffs never make things that easy! Fawn mated to fawn will normally only produce fawn puppies. The exceptions can be where one of the fawns is actually a very pale apricot (often the key can be spotted on top of the head where a true apricot colour can be detected), in which case you can have apricots in the litter. Brindle to brindle matings can result in any combination of brindle puppies (silver-fawn brindles or apricot-brindles), and can also produce both fawn and apricot puppies. This is decided wholly by the background genetics of the two parents; if there is fawn, and/or apricot in the background of the parents, puppies of these colours can occur

in the litter. Apricot to fawn matings will produce both colours in the litter, unless, again, the fawn is actually a pale apricot, in which case you would get mostly apricot puppies, but fawns can still occur. Apricot to apricot should most likely produce apricot puppies, but the apricot colour is the most difficult to understand, and you could end up with fawn puppies.

THE BROOD BITCH

Is my bitch good enough in looks and in temperament to breed from? *This is the first, and most important question you should ask yourself when planning a litter.* If you have been showing your bitch with some success, no doubt some of the judges and fellow exhibitors will have passed comments and opinions on her. This is fine as far as it goes, but you must be confident that these people really know what they are talking about. There are always far too many 'instant experts' who may try to encourage you to breed from a bitch that may, in fact, be inferior in some way. They may also be just as quick to suggest a stud dog that is supposedly 'ideal'.

However, if several knowledgeable Mastiff owners agree that your bitch does have qualities which should be brought forward, look hard at her again before making the final decision. The chances of producing a good litter from an inferior dog and/or bitch are very slim indeed. In fact, the chances of producing a very ordinary litter from super parents are high enough – such is the unpredictability, and the thrill, of breeding. If you decide that your bitch is just not good enough, she will still be a faithful companion throughout her life.

You may decide to have her spayed (sterilised). This is a comparatively simple but major operation which obviously means the bitch no longer has normal seasons, but you may find that a couple of times a year she will show some of the behaviour patterns she used to show before being spayed. This is due to some continuing hormonal activity, but causes no real problems. She may still tend to have phantom pregnancies. Your vet may say this is impossible since it is the ovaries which produce the hormones and these are normally removed, but it really does happen, and any vet with his feet on the ground should accept this. In the same way, some bitches can show tremendous behavioural changes, especially in temperament, which are exactly the same as in the recently whelped bitch. Again, this is caused by the hormone activity and changes as the body settles down to the 'normal' after a period of complete change.

THE STUD DOG

The stud dog owner must also think seriously before allowing their dog to mate a bitch. Firstly, is the dog genuinely good enough to use for breeding? Has he, or his

Ch. Parcwood W. Bear Esq of Lesdon.
This dog proved to be an outstanding sire,
and his name is featured on many
pedigrees in the UK and overseas.

Pearce

siblings, shown any undesirable faults in conformation or in temperament? Can he offer anything special to the breed? Do you have the set-up to provide a home for an active stud dog? It may seem impossible that the quiet, gentle lounger in front of the fire could turn into a persistent sex maniac. While the majority of dogs continue as they were before being used at stud, a good proportion of dogs will undergo a complete change in their nature. This type will become 'all dog', seeking out bitches in season, and then, if such a bitch is located, the dog will howl, attempt to break down doors and even leap over gates and fences in his efforts to get to the bitch. So be warned!

Occasionally, a young dog may tend to 'hump' at objects, or someone's knee. This

Ch. Vi Et Armis Unanimous Verdict (Ch. Gildasan Roman Warrior – Ch. Vi Et Armis Karla A. Fatori): a successful show dog and a sire of Champion offspring.

is a natural part of growing up, but it can become a nuisance and it is best to gently scold the dog and stop him from doing it. This is much easier to do while he is young, stopping him at the first signs. Above all, do not make a great fuss, or he will become confused, and if you eventually decide to use him at stud, you may find he remembers being reprimanded, and will not perform when required. Dogs do tend to mark their territory, including around the house! This can be prevented with a little scolding, but the stud dog may have more of a tendency to do this, especially if other dogs or bitches visit his home.

If you decide against using your dog at stud, do not expect a miracle cure to all known behavioural problems if you have him castrated. Do not believe the vet who

A winning line typified by Ch. Mistletoe Bella, a daughter of Ch. Vi Et Armis Unanimous Verdict out of Ch. Walnut Hill Reminiscence.

Bernard W. Kernan.

tells you that castration is the only sure cure for all 'male' problems, including aggression, domination, fighting with other dogs, escaping in search of bitches, and marking territory in the house. While a castrated dog may not be able to perform a mating, he can have the behaviour patterns set in his mind to the point where the hormone activity, which normally drives such things, is totally irrelevant. The behaviour is governed by habit.

THE BITCH IN SEASON

If, after all due consideration, you have decided to try to breed a litter, the actual timing of the event will be totally dependent on the bitch's season pattern. Most

Mastiff bitches will have their first season between six and twenty months of age, and will then have seasons ranging from those with a regular six month cycle to those who come into season at very irregular times, varying from five to fourteen months apart. The answer is to keep a fairly close check when she first comes into season, and then keep careful records of her pattern and attitude each time she comes into season.

The first sign that a bitch is in season is usually a slight swelling of the vulva, which may become darker in colour. This will probably be followed by a moistening, then a change to a pale colour. When you first see the change of colour, the flow of blood will probably become quite heavy within twenty-four hours, and stay so for several days. Around nine days from the start, the colour will change slightly, becoming less prolific and rather more watery. From this time on, the showing of the watery discharge will slowly diminish and then dry up altogether by about nineteen or twenty days. This is followed by the vulva reducing to 'normal' size and colour.

Mastiffs like to make life interesting for us, however, and the above pattern is what we may call 'normal'. All bitches have slight variations on the normal, and each bitch has her own timetable for each stage of her season, which is a result of the very complicated hormone changes that happen in each stage as the uterus is prepared for an impending pregnancy, the ovaries are set to produce the mature eggs at the right time, and the sex organs prepare to accept the male. If all this sounds complicated, it is hardly surprising to find that variations are possible, and the Mastiff bitch seems to excel in showing the widest possible range.

The eleventh day of the season is generally considered the best time for a successful mating, so most breeders try a mating on the ninth day, with a repeat mating on the eleventh day, and again on the thirteenth day. In many cases this may result in a perfectly good mating, and sometimes a pregnancy, but observation of the bitch may show that she appears to be at her peak as early as the fifth day or as late as the twentieth day – and she will only produce puppies if mated at these times.

There are some smear tests and blood tests which are designed to show exactly when the bitch is ovulating, and therefore when she is ready for mating. Some breeders find these effective, whereas others find that they do not appear to work at all. Mastiffs are not the most fertile of breeds, and nature appears to be rather contrary, as those that we consider to be the best specimens often fail to produce, or give very small litters, while poor specimens seem to be quite prolific – yet another reason why it is essential to be totally honest about stock when you are planning a litter.

There is another problem which affects some breeds, and certainly affects

Mastiffs, and that is the 'blind season'. In this case, all the hormone activity seems to be at odds with outward appearances. We have both of us recorded cases where a bitch who lives with a dog shows no signs whatsoever of coming into season (sometimes she never appears to have any seasons at all), but her mate will suddenly show all the signs of her being in a very interesting condition. You check her, and there is nothing to show at all – no swelling of the vulva, and no colour – so you decide the male has lost his judgement. Then, the next thing you know is that the pair have completed a successful mating! This is a very difficult situation for the breeder, and there is nothing you can do about it. In time, you may learn that certain bitches are prone to this condition, but it makes any planned breeding a virtual impossibility.

Before you make the final decision to go ahead with a mating, you must satisfy yourself that your bitch is fit and well, because it is foolish to breed with a bitch who is one degree under, for whatever reason. Some stud dog owners will insist on the bitch also being smear tested before mating to ensure she has no infections or bacteria in her genital tract. This could affect her chances of conception, but, more important, it could infect the stud dog and either make him ill, or prevent him ever again siring puppies. This decision is one which you should respect. Similarly, some stud dog owners have their dog checked before and or after each mating for protection. Give consideration to the bitch's worming programme – most breeders prefer not to worm their bitches during pregnancy – so worming should be carried out prior to mating. Despite this puppies often do have some worms when they are wormed for their first time.

THE MATING

The only way you can say with any degree of certainty that a bitch is ready for mating is to have your own dog on the premises, but, of course, this is not practicable in most cases. If you have reason to think that a bitch is in fact in season, you can get some idea of how she would react to a dog by stroking the inside of her thigh, or the vulva itself. If she turns her tail to one side and braces herself, then she would probably accept a male. If she responds slightly, looking a little embarrassed, it is likely that she will be ready in a few days time. It really is a case of observation and perseverance.

When it comes to the mating, a stud dog needs to be experienced; he needs to understand what is required of him and be willing to co-operate. He should not have been chided when young for being 'sexy', and he should be used to being helped by his owner or handler. There is nothing worse than having a stud dog who, having mounted the bitch, gets off in a huff when an attempt is made to help him or to hold the bitch steady for him. A young dog that is going to be used at stud should, ideally, have his first bitch at about eleven months of age (the dog is usually a few months older in the USA). He should be put to a helpful and matronly bitch, and be assisted by his owner at the first attempt. He will then take such assistance for granted. A stud dog that will treat the bitch gently, and not rush her, who will thrust slowly to begin with until he actually penetrates, who does not exhaust himself, or hurt and anger the bitch, and does not rake her back with his claws, is a jewel of great price. Too many Mastiff stud dogs get themselves so worked up at the start of the operation, that they are no good to man nor beast.

As soon as you think the bitch is, or may be, ready for mating, then you should take her to the stud dog. It is better to get there too soon than too late, and it is wise to make arrangements to leave her for a few days, if possible, although of course it is always more satisfactory to see the actual mating. Introduce the dog and bitch in a quiet and confined spot – a large kennel run, perhaps, and with the bitch on a lead. If both are uninterested, you can take it that she is not ready, even if a vet has told the bitch's owner that she is ready. Betty recalls a bitch, who fortunately lived only fifteen miles away, and who was pronounced by the vet to be absolutely ready. She flew at the dog like a fiend, and he could not have been less interested. The owner thought that all was lost, but Betty insisted that it was a case of the bitch not being ready. Fortunately, the handler listened to her and brought the bitch back every other day for ten days, at the end of which the bitch stood willingly, and a good litter resulted.

If, on the other hand, the bitch does not react too violently, and lets the dog sniff her, has a sniff herself, and even wags her tail, the signs look good. Give them time, and do not expect instant results. Even if she objects to start with, the chances are that, given time and a considerate stud dog, she will decide to co-operate. When you think that the flirtation time or introductory time has gone on long enough, and if the dog is eager to mount her, it is wise to put the bitch over a soft bale of straw. This is to support her, as in most cases the dog is so much heavier than the female, and her legs may give way at the crucial moment. Until she is comfortably settled the dog should not be allowed to get too excited. Once on the bale, the dog can be encouraged to mount her.

If willing, the bitch's owner should stand at the bitch's head and hold it tightly, to prevent her turning and snapping suddenly. The stud dog's owner should kneel at the side of the bitch, with one hand under her tummy, so as to help the dog by placing the vulva on the penis. No attempt should be made to put the penis into the vulva, as this is likely to cause premature ejaculation. As previously stated, an experienced stud dog will thrust fairly gently until penetration is actually accomplished. Then he will thrust fiercely, and the stud dog owner will probably give a good push at the base of his spine and hold him into position. A word of warning: a Mastiff dog weighing 200 pounds or more, stamping heavily with his hind legs while 'working', can wreak havoc on shoes, toes and stockings, and so handlers should be sensibly equipped, wearing boots.

When the dog has penetrated and is lying along the bitch's back, her head must be held quite tightly, as this is the moment of pain for the bitch, and she may well object strongly, even if she has been quite willing up until this point. Keep them quiet, soothe them, and don't let them struggle and pull. It is advisable to let the dog lie along the bitch's back for the first four minutes or so, before turning them. Remember that the gland at the base of the penis has swollen enormously, and is inside the bitch, enforcing the 'tie', and so neither can escape the other. This is one reason why a mating should never be unsupervised, and terrible damage can be done to both, but especially to the dog, if when tied, the bitch panics and tries to flee.

After the first few minutes, if all is quiet, take the dog's front foot – the left is usually easiest – and bring it over the bitch's back. Repeat with the hind leg so that they are standing rump to rump. A 'tie' can last for anything from five minutes to forty-five minutes, or even more. Betty recalls a tie that lasted two hours – and that mating took place in an open-sided goat shed, in freezing temperatures, in the middle of a snow storm!

When the dog and bitch finally part, put the bitch away somewhere quiet, and do not let the stud dog mix with other males for a while – it might provoke a fight. If the dog is a proven stud, then one mating may be all that is necessary, but if you or the bitch's owner opt for more, then I think a couple of matings is sufficient. This ensures that there is not too long between the first mating and the last, which could cause problems if a caesarian birth should become necessary. The vet will want to know when the birth should have taken place, and with multiple matings, it is difficult to be precise.

When it comes to mating, it is important to bear in mind that a Mastiff bitch can be physically ready for mating, but mentally unready. You have to make a fine judgement between the two – how much coercion should be used? Admittedly, if she is absolutely unready, there will be no mating, coercion or not. But sometimes a bitch, who is reluctant to stand, has to accept a certain amount of forcing; it is a case of knowing how much to use. A bitch should never be forced against her will, but Mastiffs can be reluctant to play their part in the continuation of their species. It is therefore most important to get the timing just right, to give the parties time to get to know each other, and to have a gentle but persistent stud dog.

Chapter Ten

PREGNANCY AND WHELPING

This is a subject of many facets, and it is impossible to cover every eventuality in a volume such as this; there are whole books on just this one subject, although much of their material is never likely to be met in the case of Mastiffs. Due to their size, you are not too likely to cause pain or distress to the mother or to the pups if you give a little assistance at the birth.

THE PREGNANCY
An experienced owner may well be able to tell if their bitch is in whelp at about four weeks after mating, but those who are not as well informed may not be able to tell, with any degree of certainty, until much later. The period of gestation is around sixty-three days, but all bitches are different, and it is often a matter of knowing your bitch and the line she comes from, in order to anticipate the likely date for whelping. David had a bitch that always whelped on the seventieth day, with no ill effects to herself or her puppies. But in most cases, the vet should be asked to check the bitch if she goes longer than twenty-four hours past her due date.

At about five weeks after mating, you will probably see a gentle, general enlargement of the bitch's body, but if the litter is small, and the bitch is carrying the puppies high up under her rib cage, it may not be possible to be positive until almost the due date. More than one bitch has been taken to the vet for a check, and the owner been told that she is certainly not in whelp, and then she goes on to produce a healthy litter of four or even more, to everybody's amazement. With modern ultrasonic scan equipment, a good operator can tell with certainty exactly how many whelps are present, and can monitor any which die in the uterus, which makes a tremendous difference to the choices open to the owner and the vet. It must be stressed that this procedure is completely safe for the bitch and the puppies, but it does require a skilful operator.

From about five weeks, if the bitch appears to be in whelp, the normal feeds can be stepped up by adding 'good' foods such as cheese, fish and scrambled eggs, perhaps, and you can give some added vitamins and sterlised bonemeal. You can also give quite large doses of Raspberry leaves (available in tablet or powder form), which is a herbal remedy of long standing which has been found to aid easy and uncomplicated whelping. If the bitch gets very big and heavy, you should cut down the amount offered at each meal, and feed three times a day in slightly smaller quantities to avoid overloading her system.

THE WHELPING BOX

Once you are sure the bitch is in whelp, you should make arrangements for the whelping, starting with the whelping box. Experienced breeders all have their favourite style and size of whelping box, but the golden rule is that there must be ample size to allow the bitch to stretch out at full length, and to turn round. It is always best to fit 'pig rails', which are guard rails along each side, set in about six inches or even a little more from near the top of the box. This means that when the bitch lies down there is a gap between her back and the side of the box. This enables the puppies to get out of the way when mother is reclining gently, and it often prevents them from getting squashed.

A typical whelping box will measure about 6ft by 5ft, with sides about 1ft high. It helps if one side can be easily unscrewed to give a shallow side, ready for when the babies become mobile and start to wander. Wood is the long-standing favourite material for whelping boxes, but there are moulded plastic boxes now being marketed, mostly in the smaller sizes. These appear to be a bit smooth and slippery, which is not ideal, but they are obviously completely hygienic, and can be disinfected with very strong chemicals without harm or absorption.

The whelping box should be placed in a quiet and warm room; and the expectant mother should have the chance to get used to it, and she should be sleeping in it well before the due date. It is generally recommended that the whelping quarters should be somewhere out of the way, and this is normally true. However, we have both found that some bitches, especially those who are used to living in the house, will decide where they want to whelp, and will pay no attention to your plans. One such bitch refused to whelp anywhere but in the front sitting-room, and the whelping box always had to be placed in the centre of this room, where she held court! But in most cases, a quiet and peaceful place is by far the best, and certainly the whelping box

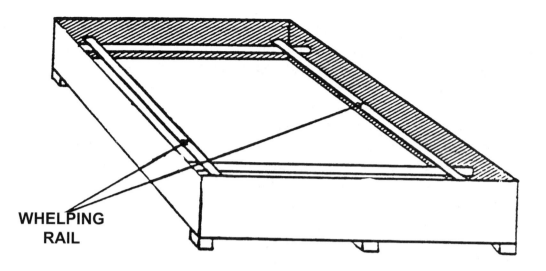

WHELPING
RAIL

The whelping box, showing 'pig rails', which
prevent the bitch lying on her puppies.

should be out of the way of young, inquisitive children. At least a week before the whelping date, make sure that the bitch sleeps in the whelping box. As the time draws near, she may get restless; she may start to dig up her bedding, and she may go off her food. On the other hand, she may do none of these things! Very often, a drop in temperature will give an indication as to when whelping is due to commence. Generally speaking, a drop from the 'normal' 101 degrees Fahrenheit to 100 degrees Fahrenheit means that the pups will arrive within about twenty-four hours; when the temperature drops to 99 degrees Fahrenheit, they should be imminent. The ideal bedding is plenty of newspapers with a rug, preferably a 'veterinary fleece', on top, and this will make a snug and hygienic bed. Ordinary rugs tend to hold dirt and soiling, whereas the fleece allows the moisture to pass through on to the newspaper underneath. The fleece can also be easily machine-washed. Be prepared for those bitches who refuse to have any bedding in the box while they are whelping. In this instance, any attempt to replace discarded bedding or newspaper will be met with a repeated throwing-out of all materials, and the bitch will happily proceed to whelp on the bare wood of the box. This may appear unhealthy, but you must allow the mother to decide what she wants, and the puppies do not appear to suffer. Indeed, there can be problems with new whelps being lost in the bedding while whelping continues. Once the bitch has finished whelping, she will usually accept some bedding, which saves bruising her elbows and hocks.

THE WHELPING

If, as we hope, you are with your bitch when she starts to whelp, you may well not notice any overt straining. Watch for the ripple of the muscles down the back, and an arching of the tail away from the body. This arching of the tail is often the only indication that a puppy is actually on the way. If, while this is happening, you place your hand in the space between the anus and the vulva, you should feel that it is enlarged and hard, with the puppy waiting to be presented. Another push, and it should emerge, complete in the membrane. If the waters have not broken prior to this, they will do so now, in a flood, so keep plenty of dry newspapers to hand. The breaking of the waters – which can happen any time from fifteen minutes or more before a puppy arrives, to the point of birth – is the discharge of the fluid which has cushioned the puppy in its individual sac during the time of pregnancy. The fluid has a greenish tinge, and a slight but distinctive odour, and varies in quantity from a small cupful to over a pint for each puppy. Hence, some bitches who appear quite full have only a couple of puppies, while others surprise us by producing a good number after appearing quite small throughout their pregnancy.

You will need to be armed with plenty of dry towelling, so that each puppy can be rubbed and dried if necessary. The bitch should do this herself with her tongue, but often she will not be quite sure what to do and you will need to help. If she makes no move, quickly break open the membrane and get the puppy's head into the air, clearing the nose so that the new-born pup can breathe. This is done by very gently cupping your hand around he muzzle and 'milking' down the length of the nose, expelling any fluid which may hamper breathing. If the puppy is not expelled by the bitch, you may need to assist in the process with your hand and towel. Do not pull at the whelp; do so in conjunction with the bitch. When she strains, you can pull gently *downwards* at the same time, but work as a pair, not separately. You can normally get a slight grip of the nose, with a dry towel – it may be the legs or the tail if it is a breech birth – and then you can help the slippery creature into the world. Incidentally, breech birth is a frequent and quite harmless phenomenon in dogs; there is usually little difficulty in delivering a breech puppy, and there is no danger to the mother or the whelp.

The afterbirth should come away at the same time; if it does, and if the bitch makes no move to bite through the umbilical cord, then you must do the job for her. This can be done by shredding the cord, well away from the body with your finger nails, or shredding in a sideways fashion. Do not try to cut the cord with scissors. Once separated from the placenta (afterbirth), the puppy should be rubbed vigorously with another dry towel, until it squeaks and air gets into the lungs. Of course, if the mother is prepared to do all this by herself, so much the better, but keep an eye on her to ensure that she is not too rough, and does not bite the cord through too near the stomach, as this can cause a hernia. Incidentally, a puppy is much tougher than many people realise, and if the whelp is slow to start breathing, you should rub it fairly roughly; do not make the mistake of being too tentative and gentle in your approach.

If a puppy is struggling to breathe, hold it firmly by the hindlegs with a hand around the back, and swing downwards, quite hard, in order to expel water from the lungs. This, coupled with more hard rubbing, usually gets things moving. Do not give up too soon. Persevere, sometimes for ten minutes or more. When the puppy is dry and breathing and squeaking, give it back to the mother for more licking and bonding. It is important to check that there is an afterbirth for each puppy, even if it does not come away at the same time. Retained afterbirths can cause problems, such as raised temperature, in the days after whelping. Many mothers will quickly eat up the afterbirths at the time they bite the cord; this is a very natural habit and the bitch should not be scolded. The afterbirths will do her no harm, but they may make her stools a bit sloppy in the next couple of days. These stools will be very dark in colour due to the richness of the afterbirth.

If the bitch seems to be progressing well, and is ready to deliver the next puppy quite soon, it is a good idea to put the previous baby into a deep cardboard box, on a well wrapped-up hot-water bottle, so that it is not endangered in any way during subsequent births. If the bitch reaches round to lick a new puppy, she could easily lie heavily on one of the earlier arrivals, or squash one with her elbow. A bitch should not go for more than two hours between delivering puppies. If this happens, it is advisable to ask the vet to check her, and, if necessary, to give her a shot of Oxytocin or some similar treatment, to stimulate the muscles and start her straining again. Mastiffs do tend to suffer from uterine inertia and a bitch may go on strike midway through whelping, perhaps through tiredness, and she may need veterinary assistance. When the last puppy has been born, and the bitch relaxes, encourage her to go out into the garden to relieve herself. When she returns to the whelping box, put all the puppies to her to nurse. If there is one puppy who is reluctant, or weak, you may need to hold that pup on to a teat to get it going. It is important that pups suckle during the first few hours of life as at this time the bitch's milk contains colostrum, which is rich in protein and contains antibodies which are essential to the puppies' well-being.

It has to be said that Mastiff bitches can be very clumsy, and we think it is essential that a new mother should not be left alone with her puppies, for quite some time. Many breeders stay with them for the first two weeks – night and day. Perhaps this is excessive, especially if the mother is experienced and known to be gentle.

Mastiffs make good mothers, but a close check must be kept on the litter for the first few days, as it is very easy for a puppy to get squashed.

A Mastiff bitch needs room to be comfortable, but the whelping box should not be so big that the puppies stray too far from their mother.

However, it is probably better to be safe rather than sorry. It would be terrible to stay with the bitch and the puppies for several days, and then to go off for a few hours sleep, and then to return and find a squashed baby. Other big dogs, even giant breeds like Great Danes, will go into a whelping box and pick their way around, gently easing themselves in without damaging the puppies. Most Mastiffs tend to rush in from the garden where you have left them while you changed the bedding, go straight into the box and lie down, FLOP, and heaven help any little thing that happens to be in the way or underneath them.

This chapter covers only the early days in the puppies' life, not their subsequent development. Do remember that warmth is essential – more puppies have died of cold than for any other reason. Keep them warm and clean, keep the mother well fed, loved and cared for, and you should see the babies grow and thrive and become personalities in their own right. All of the above must sound daunting to those unaccustomed to dog breeding, but there is a very good chance that your bitch will work things out for herself, and all you will have to do at the time of the birth is sit and watch. Litters can vary in size from one to fifteen, but most consist of about five to eight puppies.

WHELPING PROBLEMS

UTERINE INERTIA

Unfortunately, this condition is common in the breed, and if injections will not stimulate the whelping process, then you will need to consider a caesarian operation. Sometimes this becomes necessary halfway through whelping, at other times there will be no puppies born naturally and a caesarian is the only option. This is a controversial subject, but it is important not to leave it too late if a caesarian becomes essential. So many puppies die (and healthy bitches, too) because the operation has not been done in time, and then the pups, all perfectly formed, are found to be dead in the uterus because of the time which had elapsed between the time they should have been born and the time the operation was eventually carried out. We may be labelled as scaremongers, but we would never let a bitch go more that twenty-four hours overdue. After this time, a caesarian certainly gives the puppies the best chance of survival, although it is quite accepted that a bitch can, and often does, whelp perfectly naturally two or even three days after the theoretical due date. Obviously this is a subject that is governed by personal opinions, but our advice is based on many years of breeding Mastiff litters.

It is a *must*, and a big *must*, that you trust your vet, and that he or she be prepared to do what you request. After all, you are the paying customer, and will probably

know a good deal more about your chosen breed than the vet does. Before the pups
are due, discuss the possibility of a caesarian, and make sure that the vet will not
insist on leaving the bitch for several days after the puppies are due, before
operating. If your vet is reluctant to conform to your wishes, then change your vet! It
is also important to find out whether you will be allowed to be present in the
operating room. This will give you the chance to attend to the puppies, while the vet
and assistants concentrate on the bitch. Sometimes the veterinary staff are so busy
with the bitch that the puppies do not receive the immediate attention that they need.
It is therefore better to be there yourself, if it is permitted. It must be stressed,
however, that birth can be a messy business, and a caesarian may be distressing to
anyone who is unduly squeamish. If you are worried about this, it might be better to
ask someone else to assist, rather than risk feeling faint or poorly in the surgery.
From all the above, you will see that it is absolutely essential that you have a first
class rapport with your vet.

ECLAMPSIA

This is not, strictly speaking, a whelping problem, as it can occur any time after
whelping. It most frequently occurs some three weeks after whelping, and in rare
cases it can occur just prior to whelping, although this is very difficult to diagnose.
While the puppies are being formed, and while milk is being produced in large,
increasing quantities, the bitch has to draw on her calcium reserves since she often
cannot assimilate enough from her food sources. If she reduces her own reserves too
far, she will become very ill very quickly, and prompt action is needed to inject
calcium in an easily assimilated form, normally as a colloidal suspension.

The danger signals are a bitch who starts to look 'strange', often expressed as a
lost, vague look; she will be liable to flop down without warning, and there may be a
twitching of the muscles. This situation can deteriorate very rapidly until the bitch is
unable to stand and is panting heavily. This is followed by a coma, and from this
point onwards it tends to be downhill all the way. If you have the least suspicion that
your bitch may be suffering from eclampsia, contact the vet immediately. The
treatment is to inject large quantities of calcium gluconate into the bitch. If you have
liquid calcium to hand, give the bitch a good dose (a couple of tablespoonsful) every
fifteen minutes until the vet arrives. The immediate effect of the injection is
remarkable, but it is important not to let the bitch overdo it. The puppies' feed
should be supplemented, and the bitch should only feed each puppy for a minute or
so till she is fully recovered. If a bitch has suffered from eclampsia, it is essential to
keep a close watch on her in case of a relapse.

Chapter Eleven

REARING A LITTER

THE FIRST TWO WEEKS

At birth Mastiff puppies weigh about two pounds, although this can vary by quite a large margin. They will remain about the same weight for a couple of days, but once they have settled down after the trauma of arriving in this world, you can almost see them grow. However, size is not the most vital consideration during the first few weeks of life; maintenance of condition is far more important.

A healthy pup has a nicely rounded tummy that should not be blown out with milk, or with wind; it should be firm and smooth, as the puppy settles down to a pattern of feeding and sleeping. The coat should be smooth, not rough and lacking lustre, and the puppy should be quite active. Watch out for the sluggish, lethargic puppy who may not be feeding, especially if it is a bit smaller than the others in the litter. You should be prepared to sit with the litter so that you can identify any pup who appears a little under par, and then you can put that pup on to a teat while the others are either asleep, or you can remove the rest of the litter to a box for a few minutes to give the weakling a chance to feed. If the puppy remains sluggish, or fails to feed, it may be worth trying it on a little bottle feed.

All puppies are both blind and deaf at birth. At about ten days you will see a glint of light catching the gradually opening eyes, and at the same time you will notice that response to sounds starts to increase. Watch out for any eyes that appear to be gummed up; this is caused by the various secretions becoming stale and potentially contaminated. As soon as you notice a puppy with this condition, wipe the eyelids gently with a little cotton wool (cotton) soaked in a few drops of eye lotion (the human type, such as Optrex, is ideal). If this does not solve the problem in a day or so, or you are worried, speak to the vet. It is worth watching this carefully since, very occasionally, you can get bacteria such as E Coli in the eyes, which can result in problems or even blindness in extreme cases.

In Mastiffs, dewclaws are not usually removed, as is practised in some other giant breeds, and there is never a problem in later life with dewclaws catching either in brambles or such like (the normal reason quoted for their removal), nor of tearing at a bitch's flanks when the male is mating a bitch. However, a regular check should be made to ensure the dewclaws do not grow too long and curl into the leg.

TWO TO FOUR WEEKS

From the age of about two weeks, the puppies will be doubling in size approximately every eight to ten days, and they will be becoming very vigorous – much to their mother's consternation. At two weeks the puppies will also be struggling to get up on their legs and walk about. Prior to this, they are rather like slugs and move by wiggling and pushing out with their developing legs and arms. This is a very interesting stage to watch, as the puppies wobble about on their strange-feeling legs and start to play with their siblings. Most Mastiff puppies have no leg problems at this stage, but be careful that the dam does not tread on their feet, as this can damage the toes and the muscles in the legs.

Mastiffs tend to be noisy babies. When they are hungry, or being attacked by another puppy, they will bellow – and the voice of the future makes itself known! If you hear a real bellow, make sure you get to the nest quickly, in case the dam has partly sat or trodden on one of the puppies. If this happens, it is important not to panic the mother, who may respond by trampling on the whole litter. The best course of action is to talk gently to the mother, and at the same time, ease the unfortunate victim out of the predicament. Then reassure the mother and the puppies, and they will all settle down again. Mastiff mothers are a little clumsy, and will sometimes totally ignore a screaming baby. However, they are very sensitive, so always be calm and kindly. If the mother does squash a baby and you find it dead, do not scold her, as she will not understand, but simply remove the body, preferably when she is not looking.

At about three to four weeks the puppies may need to have their toe nails trimmed, as they can make a sore mess of the mother's teats. Use a small pair of human nail-scissors or nail-clippers, and just remove the very tip of the nail. If you examine the nails, you will see that they are fairly solid, with a lighter extension, usually creamish in colour, and it is this tip which you need to trim. If you try to cut the main part of the nail you will draw blood.

Ears and eyes should be checked as a matter of routine, and this serves two functions. In the long term it accustoms the puppy to being examined, and it also helps you to detect any problems at an early stage. When the puppies are suckling, some of them get milk around the eyes, which encourages bacteria to breed. The signs to look for are watery eyes, or a balding around the eyes. This condition will worsen if the bed is not kept clean and dirt builds up, and the results can be disastrous. Dust and dirt can collect in the ears, and this should be eased away by wiping with cotton wool (cotton), moistened with a little clean water or Vaseline, if necessary. *Never* probe or delve into the deeper parts of the ear, as grave damage can be caused. If the ears become foul-smelling, contact the vet, who can clean them and prescribe suitable drops to continue the treatment.

SUPPLEMENTARY FEEDING

If your puppies start to look thin, especially if you have a large litter, some supplementary feeding can work wonders. Do not split the litter and leave some with the mother, and take on some to hand rear. It is better to give one or more extra little feeds from a bottle to all the litter, and this will help the mother to cope. Use a human baby bottle and a teat with a fairly small hole. This is particularly important with young pups, as too great a flow of milk will result in the puppy choking, or the milk getting into the lungs.

The best method is to hold the pup on your knee, and lay the bottle as flat as possible, with the teat in its mouth. From time to time, remove the teat to ensure it is not blocked, and to reduce the chance of too much wind being developed. The quantity will vary depending on the age and condition of the puppy, but try to avoid the puppy ending up with a bloated tummy. It is better to give two smaller feeds than one big feed. An input of ten millilitres may well be all that a very small baby wants, but a three to four-week-old pup may take a quarter pint at one go. However, hopefully by this stage the puppies will be lapping from an open dish and going on to solid foods.

Milk replacer for puppies is sold under several trade names, and you may find that one brand suits your puppies better than another (this may also be a question of the water that is used in its preparation). If the puppies show any tendency to have loose stools either reduce the quantity, weaken the mix slightly, or change brands. Follow the manufacturer's directions exactly, especially with very young puppies, or you may end up with a mixture which is too rich, or too weak; either of these can be very bad for the puppies, causing dehydration or diarrhoea. Make sure that you always boil the water thoroughly, and leave it to cool to just above blood heat before mixing and feeding. Cow's milk is not at all suitable, as the balance of the various elements suits calves – not puppies! This is equally true of baby foods, which are specially designed for human babies. Dehydration can be diagnosed simply by picking up the surplus skin on the back of the neck, and then releasing it. A healthy pup's skin will reform to natural shape almost instantly, but if it stays in a raised peak, this indicates probable dehydration. The cure is basically to increase fluid intake. A little glucose in water between feeds is very acceptable, but if dehydration has been caused by loss of body fluids due to diarrhoea, you may need to add electrolytes, which can be obtained from your vet. This will re-establish the balance of minerals and fluids in the gut, and so restore the puppy's ability to absorb the nutrients contained in the food.

ORPHAN PUPPIES

Orphan puppies can be reared right from birth with a little care and a great deal of devotion! If there has been no suckling, you need to input some colostrum This can be obtained from the mother, or you can use one of the synthetic colostrum mixes, available from your vet. The colostrum is part of the development of the immune system, and assists the transition of the puppy's metabolism from the uterus to the open world, and is therefore essential for successful rearing.

Some breeders find that a foster mother is the perfect substitute if they are left with orphan puppies. A foster mother may be able to provide the colostrum, if she has just whelped a litter (if not, the substitute must be used), and she will hopefully carry on nursing the puppies as though they were her own. The difficulty is finding a bitch with milk, just at the right time. Your vet may know of a puppyless mother in the neighbourhood who would be prepared to take on a hungry litter. Again, a lot of time is needed to ensure the bitch accepts the babies and continues to accept them.

If you are going to hand rear the puppies from birth, you will have to be prepared to feed them every two to three hours, right round the clock. We find it is best to work a shift system, doing alternate shifts, for a litter of six babies takes at least an hour to feed and toilet – but even though it is gruelling, it is well worth the effort.

Puppies that are nursed by their mother receive a thorough cleaning at very regular intervals, especially around the rear end. This is essential to stimulate the puppy into doing its toilet, and you will see the puppy commence to urinate and defecate under the influence of the licking. In the case of orphans, you must substitute this source of stimulation, by wiping the puppy's rear end with a little, soft cotton wool. When this achieves the desired result, remove the soiling with a tissue, or with more cotton wool.

If the puppy appears to be a little red and sore in this area, keep the area clean and dry, using a little warm water and dabbing dry. In extreme cases, you may need to apply a little mildly medicated talcum powder, as used for human babies. Another useful human aid is baby wet-wipes for gently cleaning soiled, tender skin.

Once you have fed a puppy, don't forget to 'burp' it. This should be done by holding the puppy upright, and gently patting its back. Employ a slight up and down motion until a healthy burp is produced. It is obviously helpful to wean orphans on to solids at a fairly early age, but beware of doing so before the puppies are properly able to deal with them. When they are introduced, it should be in very slow stages, just a little at a time, and this will avoid tummy upsets.

WEANING

Weaning is the period of changing over from a milk diet to solids, and eventually on to junior versions of the adult diet. There are several methods based either on traditional meat feeding, or on the modern all-in-one complete feeds, manufactured by one of the well-known and reliable dog food companies. This is a matter of personal preference. We both like to start on best-quality finely-minced steak, in very small quantities, and gradually add meals of a puppy food (increasing in size), made up as a porridge per the instructions.

Do not expect to place a dish of meat or puppy food in front of a litter and hope to see them eat it in an orderly fashion. Remember the human babies you know! At first, it is better to sit the puppy on your lap and put a little rolled up ball of food in your palm, and place this under the puppy's nose. There is a good chance the pup will soon learn to eat cleanly, but food is likely to end up everywhere until the puppy gains the idea, at which time you can try a dish. Do watch out for some of the litter becoming expert more quickly, leaving the others sitting there puzzled and wondering what to do. Help the backward ones to feed, but above all, see that they *all* get some food.

Again, some puppies eat much more than others in the same litter, but so long as they all seem fit and healthy do not worry unduly. Start with one small meal a day, quickly increasing the frequency until the puppies are having five or six meals in the twenty-four hour day. These should be spread out to include a late night feed and an early morning feed. Six meals at five weeks is fine, and then these should be reduced slowly so that the puppies are getting five meals a day when they are eight weeks of age. From the earliest age, fresh water should be available in a shallow dish. This should be changed very regularly, and the dish washed out frequently to keep contamination at bay.

Every breeder has their own ideas, but a rough timetable for weaning should be:
EIGHTEEN TO TWENTY-ONE DAYS: Solids should be introduced – the exact timing depending on whether the litter tends to be backward or forward in its development. Steadily increase quantities as the puppies get bigger.

Puppies aged three weeks, the result of a mating between Ch. Ramuncho des Verts Tilleuls and Lesdon Lady Betteresse of Namous.

The same three puppies aged eight weeks. Pictured left to right: Uhannah of Namous, U' King Kong of Namous and Ulysses of Namous.

FIVE WEEKS: By this stage the mother can be taken away for some part of each day, perhaps returning to the litter at night for a while.
SIX WEEKS: This is a good age to remove the mother completely.
EIGHT WEEKS: The puppies should be fully weaned and independent, and ready to go to their new homes. In winter months, it may be preferable to wait until the puppies are nine to ten weeks of age.

Uhannah of Namous pictured at four months.

U' King Kong of Namous at seven and a half months.

WORMING

Worming is an important detail in rearing a litter, and a routine should be established to ensure that when the puppies leave the nest they are fit and healthy and free of worms. At about three to four weeks give the first treatment, using a roundworm wormer suitable for very young puppies. The puppies should be wormed again twelve to fourteen days later. If worms are seen in the stools, worm again fourteen

Mastiffs have widely varying growth rates, as illustrated by Namous Mistress Madalene (Junior Warrant) an early maturing type pictured at sixteen months.

Alan Walker.

The slower maturing type: Farnaby Fortune Teller of Masnou pictured at eighteen months.

Alan Walker.

*Zorba de la-Susa, pictured with Chris Eraclides. This dog has earned a place in the
Guinness Book of Records as the heaviest dog in the world, weighing 315lbs. He is
also the biggest canine earner, taking over from Lassie: he grossed £1.7 million
($2.5 million) from the film Incredible Zorba.*

days later. If if no worms are seen this time, worm again twenty-eight days later. We
normally worm every twenty-eight days until the puppies are six months of age.

THE JUNIOR DIET

Quantities of feeds are very difficult to quote, since it varies widely depending on
the particular puppy, appetite, and the food being fed. If you are using a proprietary
complete feed, follow the manufacturer's directions, but do not stick too tightly to
the quantities they may quote. Aim for a young Mastiff which is *fit not fat*. You
should not quite be able to see the shape of the ribs, but even worse is the puppy
who has great rolls of pure fat all over the body. Too much weight can so easily lead
to problems caused by the muscles not being able to support the excess weight.

Various tables of 'correct weights' have been published, but these tables should be viewed as an average. If your Mastiff looks in good condition, correctly bodied for its size and similar to others of similar breeding, do not worry. If in doubt, talk to your breeders, who will know whether their lines are fast or slow to develop and mature.

We have collated the following chart giving approximate weights, following through the growth of a Mastiff. This must be issued with a warning, because Mastiffs grow at very widely varying rates, depending on the bloodlines, and on whether it is a dog or bitch. Use the chart as a very rough guide only; if you find that your puppies are a long way different, either over or under, there is probably nothing to worry about at all. Have a word with an experienced Mastiff breeder, who will be able to tell you whether the lines you are using are slow or fast growing, fast or slow maturing lines. It is quite possible to have a puppy twice the listed weight, or half that listed, and yet there is nothing wrong with either the puppy or the chart. In the same way, once fully matured and developed, the lightest of these two dogs may end up the heavier adult.

A Mastiff is a slow maturing breed, but some lines are well known for being extremely slow to develop, while others are so mature at twelve months that they have reached almost their full final adult weight. In Britain today, it is well known that most Farnaby and derivatives, including the Namous/Masnou lines, are slow to mature. On the other hand, the Bredwardine lines and their derivatives tend to gain adult weight by about a year old. However, in final adulthood, there is almost no difference in the final size and weight, despite the widely varying growth patterns of these lines. Between these two extremes there is a wide range of other bloodlines, each having its own particular growth pattern.

MASTIFF WEIGHT CHART

Age	Dog	Bitch
8 weeks	29lbs	24lbs
9 weeks	33lbs	29lbs
10 weeks	36lbs	32lbs
11 weeks	40lbs	36lbs
3 months	45lbs	39lbs
4 months	60lbs	50lbs
5 months	80lbs	65lbs
6 months	100lbs	80lbs

7 months	125lbs	90lbs
8 months	140lbs	100lbs
9 months	155lbs	110lbs
10 months	165lbs	112lbs
11 months	170lbs	115lbs
12 months	175lbs	120lbs
13 months	180lbs	122lbs
14 months	185lbs	125lbs
15 months	188lbs	125lbs
16 months	189lbs	125lbs
17 months	190lbs	127lbs
18 months	192lbs	127lbs
2 years	205lbs	135lbs
30 months	210lbs	140lbs
3 years	215-225lbs	155-180lbs
4 years	220-230lbs	160-190lbs
5 years	220-235lbs	170-200lbs

Record known weight for a male (*Guinness Book of Records*) 315lbs

NB Weight should be formed from bone and muscle, and never from fat and flab. Care should be taken not to increase the weight of puppies unnaturally; excess weight leads to an increased likelihood of premature death.

SELLING THE PUPPIES

Responsibility is a word that we have stressed throughout the chapters on breeding and rearing, because when you have brought a litter into the world, you are responsible for every puppy in the litter, you are responsible to the breed itself and also to future generations of Mastiffs.

Before you mated your bitch, you will have probably had a number of friends saying they would love a Mastiff just like yours, and would like to purchase one of your litter. When the time comes, there will probably be a thousand reasons why they do not really want a puppy at that particular time. Do not be disappointed; it is much better to search out enthusiasts who really do wish to be owned by a Mastiff.

There are two main avenues for selling your litter. The most obvious is to advertise either in one of the various periodicals specialising in dog affairs, or in general advertisement papers. The other method, which has much to recommend it, is by personal introduction. In most countries there is a club for Mastiff enthusiasts, and often they maintain a register of those members who have puppies. In some countries this consists of a list of 'Recommended Breeders', and it is an honour and a responsibilty to be included on the list; elsewhere, often due to legal implications, the list is made up without any implication of the status of the breeder. In any case, it is up to the prospective buyers and breeders to check each other's credentials, so that the breeder is sure that the new owner will love and look after the puppy in accordance with the instructions which they will be given.

Do remember that not all prospective owners are caring serious people; some may think of a Mastiff as a status symbol, or be taken in by the appeal of the puppies. Give every potential buyer a thorough questioning to ensure that they are suitable to take care of one of the puppies that you have lovingly reared. Equally, it is the breeder's responsibilty to help clients to think through the idea of owning a Mastiff, and to point out all the pitfalls, reminding them of the responsibilities they would be taking on if they purchased a puppy.

Once you are satisfied that the new home will be suitable, the transaction can go ahead. But do not rule out the possibility of visiting the prospective purchaser's home, if you are at all uncertain as to its suitability. Do not be afraid to say *no* if there is the slightest doubt in your mind. Assuming that you are fully satisfied, it is then your responsibilty to ensure that the buyers receive all the help needed to raise and train their Mastiff puppy.

A full and detailed diet sheet should be given, showing exactly what the puppy has been fed on so far, and the programme which you would follow as the weeks and months go by. Offer tips on those little things which are so easy to forget, such as the tendency to feel that the puppy (now weighing five stones or more) "ought to know better how to behave". It is vital to remember that a twenty-week-old Mastiff is still only a puppy, despite the size, and doing something puppyish and naughty is only natural.

Make sure the buyers know how to contact you, with your telephone number prominently stated on the paperwork, and stress that whenever they are in doubt about absolutely anything, they must call you. You may not be amused when a new owner rings you very late at night with what appears a trifling question, but they obviously have a worry, and it is up to you to be available to help them. The responsibility does not end when the puppy leaves the breeder's home.

Chapter Twelve

HEALTH CARE

FIRST AID

Like any breed of dog, Mastiffs can fall foul of minor ailments or slight injury, which can easily be dealt with at home. The following is not intended as a comprehensive coverage of every accident or ailment that may occur – and your Mastiff may go through life without any mishaps – but it gives a general guide so that the dog owner knows the best course of action to follow.

ANAL GLANDS

These glands rarely cause problems in Mastiffs, but if your dog is constantly licking around the anus, or there is a foul smell, especially after passing a motion, ask your vet to check the anal glands. These are the 'territory marking' glands situated just inside the anus, and they excrete a little of a foul smelling substance, particularly when passing a motion. However, if they become infected they will be very painful, and the smell becomes worse and more constant. The treatment usually consists of squeezing out the excess secretion, and a course of antibiotics if infection is present. Your vet may show you how to squeeze the glands, if he feels you are competent to do so.

CUTS AND GRAZES

Treat minor cuts as you would for a human. Bathe with slightly salted water (most human antiseptics are too strong for a dog), and keep the cut clean. Dry the area, and sprinkle with a little wound powder if the wound is deep, in order to fight infection. In the case of serious deep cuts, these will normally need to be stitched by the vet, and the quicker this is done, the better the chance of a clean quick healing. If bleeding is pumping and bright red, indicating artery damage, it may be necessary to apply a tourniquet if the cut is on a limb. The idea is to slow down the flow of blood from the heart. You can use a rope, a handkerchief, or a belt of cord, and loop it round the limb several times, leaving room to insert a pencil or small stick, ensuring that the tourniquet is placed on the side of the wound nearest the heart. Turn the stick to tighten the tourniquet till the flow of blood slows and stops.

If the bleeding is slow and dark in colour, it is a vein which is damaged, and the tourniquet must be placed beyond the wound, stopping the return of blood from the extremity of the wounded limb. It is most important to loosen the tourniquet every ten minutes or so for at least half a minute, to allow fresh blood to flow to the cells and tissues cut off by the tourniquet. First Aid classes will assist you to do this, both for dogs and humans. Once you have controlled the bleeding, it is essential to get the dog to the vet with all speed.

DAMAGED TOENAILS

These can be a problem, since a damaged toenail may bleed profusely. If the nail is just broken back badly, check that it is not hanging and catching on everything, and then gently bathe it in salt water. With any luck, there should be no need for further action, except to keep a check as the nail regrows, and trim it to the correct shape, if necessary. If a nail is torn right out, bathe it and put on a bandage to keep it out of dirt, which could lead to an infection. Change the bandage regularly, and keep it dry. Put a plastic bag on the whole foot when the dog goes out for toilet. This injury is very painful so be very gentle as you tend the wound. A little wound powder from the vet will keep the injury-site clear of infection and it should soon heal. Depending on whether the root has been damaged, a new nail may or may not appear in a few weeks. If you cannot stop the bleeding at the time of the accident, you may have to take the dog to the vet to get the wound cauterised.

ELBOWS AND KNEES

Many Mastiffs will get bursas or large sore-looking growths on the elbows and/or knees. These are caused by pressure, and it is nature's way of protecting the joint area. It starts off as a fluid-filled capsule, and this will tend to harden in time to make a pad of tissue, which cushions the joint when the dog lies down on a hard surface. Concrete and wooden kennel beds or floors are obviously hard. Nylon carpet may appear soft, but is actually very hard to the dog's body (that is why such carpets last so long!).

There have been many suggested potions to clear these rather unsightly growths, but most do not have any real effect, especially in the adult. Incidentally, many puppies get a bursa on the elbows as a result of juvenile playing in the nest, and these normally clear and go away within a few weeks, although a little swelling may remain for some time. One thing to avoid is surgery, since the result is going to be a wound in an area which will be extremely difficult to heal. In the case of a puppy, there is a grave risk to the joint itself if the surgeon's knife cuts any of the wrong tissue. The best advice is to leave well alone. You can try applying a little surgical spirit, so long as the skin is not broken, but there is little else to be done.

EYES
Some Mastiffs have sensitive eyes, and draughty or windy conditions, or dust and seeds getting into the eyes, may cause problems. Gently wipe away any excess soiling around the eyes, and check that there are no foreign bodies in the eyes. If they appear a little sore and bloodshot, a few drops of a human eye lotion (such as Optrex) will give relief and keep the surface in good condition.

INSECT BITES
Treat as you would for humans, especially if you know what species attacked your dog. Most bites are not serious, but they can be painful, so a pain-killing potion may be required. The most serious, which will require urgent attention from the vet, is a bite in the mouth from a wasp or a hornet. These can affect breathing and even lead to death, so it is essential to get your dog to the vet as quickly as posssible so that he can administer an antihistamine injection.

FRACTURES
There is nothing that you can do if your dog breaks a bone, as it is a job for the vet, requiring X-rays and then expert setting. It is most important is to keep the dog as still as possible, and try not to move the affected bones as you transport the dog to the vet. If your vet is very near, call him and he will tranquillise the dog if he thinks fit, and he will have a stretcher to get the dog to the surgery. Try to get assistance, so that one person can stay with the dog , while someone else telephones for help. If you have to move the dog yourself, make a stretcher-like bed to move the dog on to, and then try to keep the dog as flat as possible while you get to the surgery.

HAEMORRHAGE
Haemorrhage from any orifice must be taken seriously, and urgent veterinary attention is vital. There is no simple first aid; do not try to plug the offending orifice, just get the dog to the vet as quickly as possible.

DISCHARGES

Any unusual discharge from any of the body orifices needs investigation; some are quite normal, others may indicate hidden problems either present or developing. Vaginal discharges are often present; many bitches produce a slight creamy discharge after their seasons, and providing this is not excessive, nor smelly, all is normal. However, if the discharge seems abnormal, it is advisable to get your bitch checked in case infection is present. Around the time for mating, some bitches produce a slippery fluid as an aid to mating. This is normal, but it should not be excessive. If a bitch has been mated there is likely to be a moistness for a day or two, but if an evil-smelling creamy discharge starts, this is a sign of infection and treatment is needed. It may help if you wash the area gently with a little warm water and a very little antiseptic, but antibiotics may be needed. Never attempt to mate a bitch who has any abnormal discharge, unless this has been checked by a vet who has taken a swab and declared it clear of bacteria.

After whelping, some messy bloody discharge is quite normal, and this can last for up to four weeks in some cases. So long as the discharge is not foul-smelling, all should be well. However, a pinkish creamy discharge, often but not always foul-smelling, indicates infection in the uterus, and will need urgent antibiotic treatment. If this is left untreated, a hysterectomy may be the only way to save the bitch's life. Pyometra, as it is called, can occur at other times. There may be little if any discharge, but you may detect a strong objectionable odour, traceable to the vaginal area. The vet should be contacted to advise on treatment.

Discharge from the penis is not unusual, and is part of the normal body cleansing process. However, if the discharge is excessive, or appears unhealthy, treatment may be needed Again, never attempt to mate a dog with a serious discharge until he is declared healthy by the vet. Rectal discharge is likely either to be due to anal glands, or it can be a sign of some bowel disorder or infection. Bleeding from the anus is a serious matter. It can be caused by tearing, caused by stones or other items eaten, but it can be an indication of major problems in the bowels, and the vet must be consulted. Black motions indicate the presence of blood in the higher areas of the digestive tract, and the cause should be traced if at all possible.

TAILS

If you have a great tail-wagger, there is some chance that the tail-tip will become damaged. In many cases the answer is to move a piece of furniture on which the tail is constantly caught. Try to make sure that the dog avoids rough surfaces in kennels or around the garden, which are at tail height, and try to keep the dog calm when it is in the confines of the car.

If the tail-tip persists in being damaged and bleeding, try first aid, such as a bandage which will prevent further damage, and give the tail a chance to heal. However, it is better to avoid softening ointments or creams as these rarely assist the healing process. We would recomend applying a little surgical spirit, which will help to harden the tip and a slight callus will probably form, which will absorb the knocks in future. In severe cases you will need to protect the tail, and this should be done by fixing a short piece of plastic plumbing tube to the tail, using adhesive tape. Do not expect the bandage to last for long, as your Mastiff will almost certainly chew it, but hopefully it will give the tail a chance to heal and dry up.

If this fails, there may be no alternative but to have the tail amputated, especially if the tail becomes infected. Discuss this with the vet, but, in general, it is better to have the bulk of the tail removed down to a four or five inches stump. If the vet removes just a few inches of the damaged tail, the length remaining will still be quite capable of slashing around, and healing will be a slow and difficult process.

CANINE DISEASES

Mastiffs are normally a healthy breed, and they are no more likely to pick up any particular ailment than any other breed of dog. However, it is important that the dog owner should be aware of canine diseases and hereditary conditions, so that veterinary advice can be sought at the earliest stage if a dog appears to be ailing. If your Mastiff seems quiet and is not eating well, you can suspect that something is wrong; the dog may also have a hot nose, and appear to be generally under the weather. In these circumstances, it is always wiser to contact the vet sooner rather than later. Early treatment is always more effective, and especially in the more serious ailments.

Hereditary conditions refer to problems which are passed down through the generations, although certain conditions can skip a generation and reappear at a later stage. All breeders should be honest with prospective puppy buyers and tell them of any known trouble-spots in the family history. If all breeders did this, much heartache would be saved, and the breed would be better for it. Even if the likelihood of a condition occurring is very small, it is better to be forewarned than to come across a problem 'by accident'.

Currently, there is a lot of discussion about autoimmune deficiency, where the dog's immune system does not defend itself against attack, and where the defence system in the animal's body seems to break down. To date, there is very little known about this condition, and there appears to be no evidence as to whether this is a hereditary problem or an acquired condition. We do not know of any cases affecting Mastiffs, and all we can suggest is that if you suspect your dog may be a victim, because you see many and varied symptoms and your dog is always under the weather, never appearing 100 per cent fit, then go and discuss the matter with your vet. It is important to have a vet that you trust – one that you find easy to talk to – and you will hopefully receive honest help and advice. Inevitably, you will learn more with experience, and in time, you will be able to come to your own conclusions as to what is really serious, and what is just a minor short-term spell of being one degree under.

INFECTIOUS DISEASES
All puppies should have a full inoculation programme, and this prevents the worst canine diseases from occurring.

DISTEMPER and HARDPAD: Thankfully, these diseases are very rare nowadays thanks to wholesale inoculation. Distemper is linked to measles, and where you get an outbreak of measles in children, you may find a distemper epidemic among the dog population. This is one reason why a temporary shot of measles vaccine can be given to young puppies prior to their normal injection, if your vet thinks it necessary. With some modern vaccines the puppies can be dosed quite early in their life with the full vaccination so as to gain some protection as early as possible.

LEPTOSPIROSIS and HEPATITIS are two other diseases that modern vaccines have almost eradicated. They affect the liver – leptospirosis is similar to jaundice in humans. The organisms causing most problems are present in the excreta and urine of infected rats, so it is essential to keep your premises free from infestation, and to cover all food stocks securely. Hepatitis is not thought to be the same virus as in humans. In dogs it causes extreme thirst, loss of appetite, diarrhoea, anaemia and fever. Treatment with antibiotics may help, but both diseases are extremely serious and the prognosis is not often favourable once a dog is infected. Obviously, the vet must be consulted to ensure correct diagnosis and treatment.

PARVO VIRUS This terrible disease has been brought under control with inoculations, but it is still a problem that can strike, often with devastating results. Parvo is similar to an extreme gastro-enteritis, and any dog suffering from this virus needs veterinary attention urgently. The animal vomits, suffers severe diarrhoea, and dehydrates rapidly. It is not a condition that you can attempt to treat without veterinary help, although round-the-clock nursing and the administration of fluids are essential. Additional treatment includes antibiotics to clear infections in the gut, and medicine to soothe the delicate lining of the insides. Yoghurt of the live variety can be very useful in re-establishing the natural balance in the digestive tract, once the prime problems of dehydration and infection have been removed. In any case, there is the strong chance that this balance will be upset where antibiotics are used, since the drugs also kill off the natural bacteria in the gut, and yoghurt is again recommended as part of the convalescence.

TONSILITIS: Mastiffs can be prone to tonsilitis when they are young, and sometimes when a puppy will not eat it is because it has a sore throat, and it hurts to swallow. If you suspect this, open the mouth, and hold the tongue down with two fingers held flat, and look for red swellings at the base of the throat. If these are present, the vet will normally find it necessary to give a course of antibiotics.

SKIN CONDITIONS
Mastiffs can suffer from skin problems, like any other breed, and some Mastiffs are very allergic to fleas. One flea, literally just one flea, can get the animal biting itself raw. Routine care is required to keep your dog free from parasites, but if spraying and bathing (including bedding) do not do the trick, it may be that the dog has an allergy to something such as dust or mites, and again the vet should be consulted. A simple skin test (called a scrape) can easily diagnose the presence of any foreign bodies, or selective sample strips can show what is causing the problem.

ECZEMAS
These are a group of skin conditions with a multitude of root causes. These can be irritations of the skin, such as those caused by fleas, or the result of an internal problem, where a food allergy or some other imbalance in the metabolism of the dog causes dry or wet patches on the skin, and the hair tends to fall out. It is useful to find out the basic cause, if possible, before treating the affected areas. These areas will be extremely irritating for the dog, who will scratch or bite, causing great red patches. Your vet is likely to prescribe antibiotics to get rid of the infection, and a surface treatment to kill the bacteria on the skin. It may be necessary to shave the affected area, but the coat will grow again as soon as the bugs are gone. Hydrogen Peroxide solution is suggested by some vets, and it has certainly worked in many cases.

BLOAT and TORSION
This is possibly the most common cause of premature death in Mastiffs. We speak from first-hand experience when we say that gastric torsion is a nightmare. It is caused by the build-up of gas within the stomach, and then the whole stomach

appears to twist, so that it is sealed at both ends – like a hammock that has been swung over. Another way to visualise this condition is to imagine a party balloon that is filled with water making it impossible to twist about. When it is filled with air, you can twist it about to make weird creatures, and this is exactly what happens to the stomach; but for the stomach it is not the finish. With nowhere to escape, the gas builds up, and pressure on the heart causes an agonising death. The only remedy is surgery, and prompt surgery. It does not matter if a dog becomes ill in the middle of the night, you must ring the vet immediately, explain the situation and rush your dog to the surgery for an emergency operation – *a delay of thirty minutes can be fatal*. It is still not really known why bloat occurs, although it seems to be the deep-chested, large breeds that are most commonly affected. Some people say that it is caused by food swelling in the digestive tract; others say that emotional distress can trigger an attack. There have been articles and research galore on the subject, but no one has produced a theory which covers the variety of cases. There are some things you can do to lessen the chances of bloat occurring, such as feeding two smaller meals a day, rather than one large meal. You should never let your dog take vigorous exercise after eating, and do not feed last thing at night before putting the dog to bed. An attack nearly always takes place about one to two hours after eating, so feed earlier during the day, so that you can keep an eye on the animal after the meal.

Once you have seen a case of bloat you will always remember the symptoms. The dog is restless, slobbers, and tries to vomit but cannot. Even as you watch, the stomach slowly swells until it looks like a pillar box. The stomach is tight like a drum, and, in fact, it sounds like a drum if it is tapped, because the skin is so tightly stretched. As stated, surgery, and prompt surgery, is the only treatment that will save the dog, but this is not always successful, as internal organs may have been damaged. Some breeders feel it is almost kinder to put the animal to sleep in order to avoid the major surgery and any further suffering. Again, this is not an hereditary condition, but it does seem that certain bloodlines within the breed are more prone to it than others.

CANCER
All breeds of dog can suffer from cancer; in the large breeds, especially bone cancers. Sadly, this is often fatal, but treatment is improving all the time, and, with new drugs, there are cures, or at least remissions. Again, veterinary help is required as soon as the condition is diagnosed.

CRUTIATE LIGAMENT TROUBLES
This is the most common form of lameness in dogs, and it affects the ligament

which is in the dog's 'knee'. If this ligament is stretched or torn, it causes pain and lameness. This is not an hereditary condition as such, but it appears that certain bloodlines are more prone to it than others. It can happen so easily – the dog can be running at a leisurely pace, and turn quickly, and suddenly it is on three legs, having ruptured the ligament by the sudden twist. It can also happen if puppies play too roughly with litter mates when in the early 'teens'. This is an injury which seems to happen without any warning, and the results can be serious.

Sometimes the problem can be cured by rest alone, particularly if the ligament is just stretched or slightly damaged, but very often an operation is required, and even this is not always 100 per cent successful. Anyone interested in football will know that crutiate ligament trouble is something that can prevent the very best of players from succeeding in their profession. It may not be life-threatening as such, but it is heartbreaking nevertheless.

HIP DYSPLASIA

This is an hereditary condition where the hip joint does not fit snugly into the socket; in bad cases it can lead to lameness and painful arthritis. The trouble with hip dysplasia is that affected dogs do not necessarily pass it on to their immediate offspring, and it can jump one or more generations. There are also other dietary and metabolic factors which can affect the incidence of this condition. Diagnosis cannot be made with real certainty except by X-ray, and this is not advisable until the dog is about thirteen months of age. In the USA the Orthopedic Foundation for animals will issue a permanent number for certification, unless dogs are X-rayed after two years of age.

We would strongly advise Mastiff owners to have their stock X-rayed and hip-scored, especially if they are to be used for breeding. A dog with slight dysplasia can live normally, but should not be bred from. Severely dysplastic dogs do not always suffer pain, but usually they do, and nowadays there are procedures which can be used to help, even up to having a complete hip replacement. However, this is extremely expensive, and cases are fairly rare. Possibly, hip dysplasia is not as common as it was thirty years ago, but this is a matter of personal opinion. When dogs are hip-scored, the X-rays are taken according to a very specific pattern, and are sent for scrutiny. A score of 50 per hip is allocated – the higher the score the worse the condition. Many Mastiffs have scores of 0 and 1, or 3 and 4, and these are excellent results. The figures relate to each hip, thus one side can be a '3' and the other side a '4'.

The normal score, according to Dr Malcolm Willis (the UK's foremost expert in this field), based on the number of X-rays which have been submitted to him, is between 15 and 17, in total. Other breeds have far higher scores, but even so, if breeders X-ray and score, this 'score' should get even less.

A word of warning: some vets have only to look at a Mastiff which may appear lame, and say at once 'Hip Dysplasia', without ever taking an X-ray. It is important to insist on an X-ray before you accept the verdict. The best time for an X-ray is after the dog is twelve months old, when the hips are pretty well formed and stable.

BREED 'DEFECTS'

Commonsense is essential when dealing with all livestock, and it is possible to read too much into various breed 'defects', classing them as hereditary faults before sufficient evidence has been compiled. In France some years ago, a long-coated Mastiff puppy turned up in a litter, and it was immediately suggested that the parents of affected litters, the whole litter concerned, and the grandparents of the litter, should be barred from any further breeding, since this was considered a genetic fault. Yet, everybody knows that from time to time a long-coat does turn up, but while many may suspect where it is coming from, there is no sure line of genetic linkage in every case, and the siblings may never appear to pass it on in the next few generations. Excess zeal can destroy a breed or a breeder without any justification.

There are a number of other faults which crop up from time to time in litters, which may affect a potential show career, but are of no physical disadvantage to the dog itself. These include kinky tails (where the tail appears almost to be broken, the kink varying from a slight ripple to a right angle bend part way along the tail; long coats, which can range from a heavy coat to a real ball of fluff, and Persistent Pupillary Membrane, where the membrane which covers the eyes before birth up to when the eyes open, fails to dissolve completely – there is not sufficient evidence to prove that this is hereditary.

THE OLDER MASTIFF

Owning a Mastiff, or any dog, gives great joy, companionship and responsibility. The heartache and grief comes all too soon, however, because of the short life span of a dog compared to our own. A Mastiff will normally live to ten or eleven years of age. Those who get too fat and too heavy will often die at seven or eight years.

Some Mastiffs stay active and healthy right up to the end, but generally speaking, as with humans, they tend to slow down a little as the years catch up with them. Do not make an elderly dog do anything that it finds too strenuous; if a dog is tiring, make the walks shorter – but make sure the outings are varied and interesting. Feed more frequently, but give smaller amounts, and do not let your Mastiff get too fat. A lean dog, as long as it is not too thin, seems to live longer and have more energy than a fat dog – just like humans. Most dogs will make it clear if they want to continue their old pursuits, and they should be encouraged to do so, but when a dog wants to do less, then you should comply.

There will come a time, however much we fear it, when life for your friend is not what it was. This is not necessarily the result of a specific illness, but just a case of general old age. The hindlegs get weak, the dog cannot always get up easily, and does not appear to be enjoying what it always used to do happily. The hardest thing that you, as the owner, have to do, is to decide whether it is kinder to have the dog put to sleep. If the dog is not in any pain or discomfort, and is eating its food with appetite, and enjoys lying in the garden in the sun, then you can rest assured that the dog is enjoying life. But when none of these criteria apply, then it is the time to put your own feelings to one side and decide what is best for your friend. It is an agonising decision that we all know too well.

Do not take the dog to the vet; ask the vet to come to the house. The lethal injection can then be given in the dog's own bed, in the home that your dog knows. Do not subject the animal to a trip to a strange place, but let the deed be done peacefully at home. All this is harder for the owner than for the dog, who will know no fear. Do please, put the dog's comfort and peace before your own.

One of the distressing aspects of all this, is deciding what to do with the dog's body. Most people will not be able to dig a grave in their garden, although this is one option. It is probably more feasible to contact a pet crematorium; there are now quite a few of these, as well as pet burial grounds. Whatever you decide, you will still have to face that last journey. You owe it to your dog not to let the vet dispose of the body in a manner unknown to you.

This subject is of necessity a sad one, but think of all the years you have had, and all the happiness the dog has given you. Only you, after you have said farewell for the last time, can decide whether the joy outweighs the heartache, and whether you can face the whole cycle again with a new puppy. To buy a new puppy is not to be a replacement of the old friend. Each dog has individual character and ways of bringing us pleasure, so be very careful not to make unfair comparisons between old and new. When choosing your new friend, it may be a good idea to look for a puppy of a different colour, or opposite sex, and most certainly do not buy a particular puppy because 'he or she is just like the old one'. This is courting disaster when the little bundle turns out to be nothing like the old one, although twice as lovable.

Chapter Thirteen

BREED CLUBS AND SERVICES

Clubs are an important part of every breed, and most countries in the world have clubs for specific breeds. If certain breeds are numerically small, related breeds may be grouped together. What does a breed club do? Its most important function is linking people with a common aim and interest, and this is achieved in slightly different ways, varying from country to country.

In the UK there are two Mastiff clubs, The Old English Mastiff Club and the Mastiff Association. Their functions are based within the Kennel Club Constitution, and activities revolve around the running of shows. You may feel this is aimed at a limited part of the membership, or that there is no point in non-show owners joining the clubs, but this would be a misconception. The showing of dogs, whatever the breed, is a sport where a judge's opinion is sought regarding the various aspects of each dog in relation to the Breed Standard. This, in turn, helps breeders and potential breeders to make an appraisal of their own stock and of the other exhibitors' stock. This is of great benefit in planning future matings, so that the best available choices can be made, and potential faults spotted by the judges and breeders alike. The clubs are also engaged in the training and selection of new judges, which is a part of the continuing process of regeneration.

Judges are appointed for their knowledge of the breed demonstrated over the years, and by the quality of their dogs as seen in the ring. Some people who have many years experience and knowledge of the breed, fight shy of being the centre of the ring, judging the breed. However, in many ways, the more experienced members owe it to the newer members to pass on the benefit of their experience and knowledge, wherever and whenever possible.

Clubs also keep the members informed of new products and developments, and they can also warn of any disease or other health problems, by using the regularly published newsletters. All members have the chance to air their views on matters of current interest, either through the newsletters or at annual general meetings and social events organised by the committees. Members who feel they have an area of knowledge or expertise can offer themselves to serve on a club committee. This is hard work, but it is extremely rewarding, for it is the committees who formulate the way the club and the breed will face the future.

Most other countries have steadily formed clubs to cater for the interests of the enthusiasts of the breed. In some countries, such as France, the club caters for more than one breed, in that case the Bullmastiff, and the Club Special d'Elevage show is for both breeds. Some of these clubs are very small and almost informal, depending both on the number of members, and the regulating body which is the equivalent of the Kennel Club or the AKC. In other cases, such as Australia and New Zealand, they have catered for the two nearby areas, and have used as a model the rules of the original British club, modified as necessary to cover local matters.

The largest of all the clubs, and by a long, long way, is the Mastiff Club of America. As a separate organisation, they produce a journal which is a masterpiece, respected all over the Mastiff world, where local newsletters usually consist of just a couple of duplicated pages. In a country such as America, where there are so many Mastiffs and they are so widely spread, a good interchange of information, and passing through of club changes and rules is vital. The quantity and quality of the photographs in the club journal is superb, and this publication shows one the great benefits of being a big club.

In most countries the Breed Club is mostly concerned with the running of shows, but there should always be much more going on behind the scenes in order to provide a social and educational side for all members, as well to assist in the education and appointment of judges. The future of the breed in each country is collectively in the hands of the Breed Clubs and the Kennel Clubs, and they each have a great responsibilty.

To serve as a committee member, or officer of any club is a serious and time consuming job and it deserves the best each and everyone can put into it. This work should always be carried out for the good of the breed and for the good of the club – never in pursuit of personal advancement. Most clubs have a Code of Ethics drawn up, and it is up to the club's governing body to ensure that this is adhered to by all members. This must be done with total impartiality, strictly following the rules of procedures applicable to the country.

One area in which breed clubs are heavily involved is re-homing. Sadly, there have always been some cases where, through no fault of the dog, a new home is required, and most clubs have set up facilities for finding new homes for these unfortunate animals. It is easy to feel that if every breeder checked out the new home carefully, and every new owner had thought out the potential problems of owning a Mastiff, no dog would ever need rehoming; but the real world is far from that ideal situation. There are the cases where a person dies, or becomes incapacitated and unable to care for the dog, or where a marriage breaks up, perhaps. However, many other reasons and excuses are heard every year by the devoted officers who administer these schemes. Re-homing a Mastiff can be extremely difficult, as they are so sensitive and devoted, and anyone taking on a rescue dog must be prepared to give much love and special care to a dog who does not understand being cast out and put into a strange new home. A rescued dog, once resettled into a new home, tends to be even more devoted and caring for the new owners, and is well worth the considerable effort which may be required.

In most European countries, the breed clubs are extremely powerful. They often have the power to decide which dogs can and cannot be bred from, sometimes even choosing the partners to be mated. This has advantages in eliminating known inherited faults, provided the people making the decisions are fully acquainted with the genetics involved, and are not relying on hearsay or probabilities.

Many clubs have a Code of Ethics, designed to stop the chances of bad breeding or exploitation of the breed, which on the whole must be a good guideline. However, it is patently obvious when statistics are analysed that a large majority of the breaches are perpetrated by persons who are not members of the breed clubs, and so cannot, in most cases, be brought to task. This almost negates the intentions and good efforts of the majority of breeders.

After-sales service is important and should be provided both by the breeder, and by the clubs. If Mastiff owners have a problem, they should be able to turn firstly to the breeder of their dog, or, if the breeder cannot help, the breeder or the owner should be able to talk to the officers of the club to see if assistance can be obtained from another member who may have special knowledge.

WESTMINSTER PUBLIC LIBRARY
3031 WEST 76th AVE.
WESTMINSTER, CO 80030